READING FUNDAMENTALS

by Aileen Weintraub

GRADE

5

New York

New York

An Imprint of Sterling Publishing
1166 Avenue of the Americas
New York, NY 10036

ISBN 978-1-4114-7885-5

Distributed in Canada by Sterling Publishing Co., Inc
C/o Canadian Manda Group, 664 Annette Street
Toronto, Ontario, Canada M6S 2C8
Distributed in the United Kingdom by GMC Distribution Services
Castle Place, 166 High Street, Lewes, East Sussex, England BN7 1XU
Distributed in Australia by Capricorn Link (Australia) Pty. Ltd.
P.O. Box 704, Windsor, NSW 2756, Australia

For information about custom editions, special sales, and premium and corporate purchases, please contact Sterling Special Sales at 800-805-5489 or specialsales@sterlingpublishing.com.

Manufactured in China
Lot #:
4 6 8 10 9 7 5 3
07/17

www.flashkids.com

Dear Parent,

Being able to read and understand nonfiction texts is an essential skill that ensures success not only in the classroom but also in college and beyond. Why is nonfiction reading important? For one thing, close reading of nonfiction texts helps build critical thinking skills. Another reason is nonfiction reading builds your child's background knowledge. That means your child will already have a wealth of knowledge about various subjects to build on while progressing in school. You can feel good knowing you'll be laying the foundation for future success by ensuring that your child develops the necessary skills that nonfiction reading comprehension provides.

     The activities in this book are meant for your child to be able to do on his or her own. However, you can assist your child with difficult words, ideas, and questions. Reading comprehension skills take time to develop, so patience is important. After your child has completed each activity, you can go over the answers together using the answer key provided in the back of this workbook. Provide encouragement and a sense of accomplishment to your child as you go along!

     Extending reading comprehension beyond this workbook is beneficial and provides your child with the opportunity to see why this skill is so essential. You might read a newspaper article together and then discuss the main ideas. Or head to the library to find a book on your child's favorite subject. Remember, reading is fun. It opens the door to imagination!

Famous Faces

Mount Rushmore is a granite cliff located in the Black Hills of South Dakota. This cliff is special because the faces of four famous presidents are carved into it. Surrounded by over 1,200 acres of land, it is the largest stone monument in the entire world.

In 1923, a historian named Doane Robinson came up with an idea to create an attraction that would bring tourists to the area. He convinced a famous sculptor named Gutzon Borglum to do the project. Together they asked Congress and the president of the United States, Calvin Coolidge, to fund the project. President Coolidge agreed and chose which faces to use. He picked presidents Theodore Roosevelt, Thomas Jefferson, Abraham Lincoln, and George Washington. This was because of the important work they did during our country's early history.

In 1927, Borglum and his team of four hundred men started work. They had to remove more than 800 million pounds of stone before they could begin carving. Work on the faces didn't start until 1934. They used dynamite and air hammers to carve the faces. Air hammers are a special type of hammer that uses compressed air to carve stone. Picks and chisels were also used. The crew hung from scaffolds and slings while they worked.

Borglum died in March 1941 before the project was finished. His son Lincoln took over the work. He worked on it until October 1941 when funding ran out. This meant that work would have to stop. The presidents were supposed to be carved from the waist up, but because the project ended early, only the faces were completed.

Each president's head is equal to the height of a six-story building. Their eyes are 11 feet (3.4 m) wide and their mouths are 18 feet (5.5 m) wide. Their noses are 20 feet (6.1 m) long! If their whole bodies were carved into the cliff, each one would be 465 feet (141.7 m) tall. That's as tall as a skyscraper! Just as Doane Robinson hoped, Mount Rushmore became a huge tourist attraction. Each year, more than three million people visit this national monument.

Answer the questions.

1. Where is Mount Rushmore located?

Black Hills of South Dakota

2. What kind of rock is Mount Rushmore made out of?

Granite Cliff

3. What is the name of the sculptor who carved Mount Rushmore?

Borglum

4. What are three tools that were used to carve the faces?

Picks, Dynamite, air hammers, and chisels

5. Who are the four presidents carved on the rock?

Theodore Roosevelt, Abraham Lincoln, George Whasingron and Thomas Jefferson

6. Why were these four presidents chosen?

Because They did important things in early history

7. How high is each president's head?

Of a six-story building.

8. Who took over the project for Borglum after he died?

His son Lincoln.

9. Why did work on the project have to stop?

Because funding ran out

10. How many tourists visit Mount Rushmore each year?

More Than 3 million people

A Day to Celebrate

When most people think of Labor Day, they think of the end of summer fun. But did you know that Labor Day is a holiday that honors the hard workers of the United States? The reason for this holiday is to give Americans a day of rest from their jobs. Today, there are laws that protect the rights of workers, but this was not always the case.

The 1880s was a time known as the Industrial Revolution. New inventions and machinery meant people had to work long hours. Sometimes they worked under poor conditions. Many people worked twelve hours a day, seven days a week making very little money. Often, children as young as five years old had to work to help their families. People wanted change.

To help with this problem, labor unions began to form. A labor union is a group that helps protect the rights of workers. The unions organized strikes and quit working for their employers. Sometimes these events became violent and people got hurt or died. Other events were peaceful and led to new traditions.

On September 5, 1882, about 10,000 workers took the day off without pay. They joined together for a march in New York City. This was the very first Labor Day parade. The parade honored working people who helped our country grow and prosper. Soon, the idea of a working people's holiday caught on. Many states began to celebrate the day. Even so, it was not yet an official holiday.

In 1894, workers for the Pullman Railroad Company went on strike. They were fighting for better wages. Without the workers, the railroads could not run. The government sent troops to break the strike. The strikers were forced to go back to work. The government knew it had to do something to repair its relationship with the workers of this country. In June 1894, Congress made Labor Day an official holiday. Now it is always on the first Monday in September.

To this day, there is some disagreement about who first came up with the idea of Labor Day. Some say it was a man named Peter McGuire. Others believe that it was a man named Matthew Maguire. Both of these men worked for unions.

Labor Day is a good reminder of how hard people fought for better working conditions. Many people now celebrate Labor Day by attending parades. Others have picnics, go to the beach, or stay home and relax.

Use the words from the word bank to complete each sentence.

~~five~~	protects	troops	~~parades~~	fought
~~strike~~	picnic	~~rest~~	~~machinery~~	~~Monday~~

1. Labor Day is a day of _____rest_____ for American workers.

2. New inventions and _____machinery_____ meant people had to work long hours.

3. During the Industrial Revolution, children as young as _____five_____ had to work to help their families.

4. A labor union is a group that _____protects_____ the rights of workers.

5. In 1894, workers for the Pullman Railroad Company went on _____strike_____.

6. The government sent in _____troops_____ to break up the strike.

7. Labor Day is always on the first _____Monday_____ in September.

8. Labor Day is a good reminder of how hard people _____fought_____ for better working conditions.

9. Many people celebrate Labor Day by attending _____parades_____.

10. Other people celebrate by going to the beach, or having a _____picnic_____.

The Pledge of Allegiance

Since 1892, many schools across the country have been saying the Pledge of Allegiance. The word *allegiance* means, "loyalty." By saying the pledge we show our loyalty to the American flag. When people say the pledge, they stand up, face the flag, and put their right hand on their heart. But did you ever wonder how it came to be that we say this pledge in schools?

In 1891, a Baptist minister named Francis Bellamy accepted a job at a magazine. Part of his job was to arrange programs for schools around the country. At the time, schools across the nation were getting ready for a big celebration. It was the four-hundredth anniversary of Christopher Columbus's arrival in the New World. As part of the celebration for Columbus Day, Bellamy's boss asked him to write a salute to the flag for the children to recite.

On a hot August night, Bellamy sat down to think about what the pledge should say. He felt that the pledge should be about loyalty. It was very hard for him to come up with just the right words. Writing the one-sentence pledge took him two hours. The first time Bellamy heard the pledge recited was at a Columbus Day celebration in Boston. Four thousand students said the pledge all at once.

Since that day, the pledge has been changed four times. One change happened in 1954. Congress and President Dwight Eisenhower voted to add the words *under God* into the pledge. Some people did not like this. They felt that children should not be required to say a pledge that included the word *God*. In this country, there is a separation of church and state, or government. People are allowed to practice any religion they choose. Some people choose not to follow any religion at all. They said that adding the word *God* violated this right. Others disagreed. The argument went all the way to the New York State Supreme Court. The court ruled that the words *under God* could stay in the pledge. The court also explained that people cannot be forced to say the pledge if they don't want to. Today, the pledge is still said in government meetings and schools around our nation.

Read each question and circle the correct answer.

1. What does the word *allegiance* mean?

    a) happiness   **b)** loyalty   c) disloyalty

2. What do people do when they say the pledge?

    a) stand up   b) sit down   c) face their friend

3. Where did Francis Bellamy work?

    a) at a bank   b) at a magazine   c) at a lawyer's office

4. What was the big celebration the schools were getting ready for?

    a) Veterans Day   b) Columbus Day   c) Flag Day

5. How long did it take Bellamy to write the pledge?

    a) one day   b) two hours   c) five hours

6. How many times has the pledge been changed?

    a) one   b) six   c) four

7. In 1954, what words were added?

    a) under God   b) in God we trust   c) republic

8. In America, which two things do we keep separate?

    a) children and the pledge   b) schools and state   c) church and state

9. In this country, which religions are people allowed to practice?

    a) some   b) none at all   c) any religion they choose

10. Can people be forced to say the pledge?

    a) yes   b) no   c) sometimes

Exploring Sedimentary Rocks

Have you ever picked up a rock and wondered where it came from? Maybe you wanted to know how it was formed? The next time you go exploring, look for rocks and examine them. You might find some interesting things. Rocks come in different colors, sizes, shapes, and textures. If you look closely, you might even see layers. Rocks with layers are formed under water. These rocks are called sedimentary rocks. Sometimes these rocks are small, but sometimes they are as big as giant cliffs.

Sedimentary rocks are made up of sand, mud, pebbles, plants, and even animals. Fast-moving rivers carry pieces of rock long distances. These rocks hit each other over and over again until they are worn down. This is called weathering. As the river flows toward the sea, the rocks get smaller and smaller. They form tiny pieces, called sediment.

When the river gets close to the sea, it begins to slow down. As it slows down, it leaves the bigger pieces of rock behind. By the time the river reaches the sea, it begins leaving behind pebbles and soil. As the river enters the sea, it leaves behind the tiny pieces of sediment. The heavier rocks put a lot of pressure on the smaller pieces of sediment. Over time, they form layers on the ocean floor. The layers build and become compacted from pressure. These layers are called strata. The seawater runs through the spaces in the layers, leaving behind minerals. These minerals form crystals, which act as glue. This process is called lithification. It takes millions of years, but this is how sedimentary rocks are formed.

There are many different types of sedimentary rock. Conglomerate rocks are made up of sand and gravel cemented together. They are coarse. If the pieces of sand and gravel have sharp edges, the rock is called breccia. Sandstone rocks form when sand is cemented together. Bits of silt form siltstone, and mud becomes shale or mudstone. Limestone is formed from pieces of seashells.

Next time you are out exploring, try to identify as many rocks as you can!

What's the order? Number the events 1 to 10.

_____ The seawater runs through the spaces in the layers.

_____ The rocks hit each other over and over again until they are worn down.

_____ Fast-moving rivers carry pieces of rock long distances.

_____ As the river flows toward the sea, the rocks get smaller and smaller.

_____ The layers become compacted.

_____ By the time the river reaches the sea, it begins leaving behind pebbles and soil.

_____ The heavy rocks put pressure on the sediment, forming layers.

_____ As the river enters the sea, it leaves behind the tiny pieces called sediment.

_____ The layers build, forming sedimentary rocks.

_____ When the river slows down, it leaves the bigger pieces of rock behind.

The Declaration of Independence

The Fourth of July is a fun holiday. It's a time for barbecues and fireworks. But do you know why we celebrate the Fourth? This is the day the Declaration of Independence was adopted by the Continental Congress. This document tells us why American colonists had a right to be free from the British government. It says that all men are created equal. It also says that they have a right to life, liberty, and the pursuit of happiness.

The American colonists had been living under British rule for almost two hundred years and were forced to obey British laws. But the Americans didn't agree with many of these laws. For one, the British made them pay high taxes. The Americans protested, but the British ignored them. In 1770, the British sent troops to America to threaten the colonists. Then the British closed the port to Boston, making trade impossible. The Americans knew they were going to have to fight for freedom. In 1775, war broke out. This was the start of the American Revolution.

In June 1776, Congress chose five people to write a document saying why the colonists should be free. This document became known as the Declaration of Independence. The five men were Thomas Jefferson, Benjamin Franklin, John Adams, Roger Sherman, and Robert Livingston. Jefferson was in charge of writing the document. In it he explained why the colonists deserved to make their own laws.

In early July 1776, representatives from the colonies gathered to sign the Declaration. The first person to sign was John Hancock. He signed his name in big letters to make sure the British king would have no problem seeing it.

Now the American colonists had to win the war. If they lost, the men who signed the Declaration would be called traitors and the British government would hang them. Winning would not be easy. The British had a much stronger army and better weapons. The colonists lost many battles but did not give up. They hid in forests and fired their weapons from trees and barns. They also had a smart general named George Washington who always read the Declaration to his men before battle. This way, the soldiers would remember what they were fighting for. Against all odds, the colonists won the war. A peace treaty was signed on September 3, 1783, and the British finally recognized America as a free nation.

Read each statement. Write *true* or *false*.

1. The Fourth of July is the day the Declaration of Independence was signed. _____

2. The Declaration says that no one is created equally. _____

3. The colonies lived under British rule for four hundred years. _____

4. The British made the colonies pay high taxes. _____

5. Congress chose ten people to write a document saying why Americans should be free. _____

6. Thomas Jefferson was in charge of writing the Declaration of Independence. _____

7. John Hancock was the last person to sign the Declaration. _____

8. The British had a stronger army than the Americans. _____

9. The Americans hid in the forests when they were fighting. _____

10. George Washington read the Declaration to his soldiers before battle. _____

Martin Luther King Jr. and Civil Rights

Every year, on the third Monday in January, the nation celebrates Martin Luther King Jr. Day. Students have the day off from school, and many businesses are closed. It is a day to remember a man who helped changed our country.

Martin Luther King Jr. was born on January 15, 1929, in Atlanta, Georgia. He was a smart student and entered college when he was just fifteen years old. After college, he continued his education. He studied religion at seminary school and earned a doctorate degree. While he was in school, he met his wife, Coretta Scott. He also became a Baptist pastor in Montgomery, Alabama. King believed in nonviolence and was well respected in his community.

King believed that all people should be treated equally. He saw that African Americans were not always treated well in this country. He decided to become a human rights activist. Then he joined the National Association for the Advancement of Colored People, also known as the NAACP. This is a group that fights for the rights of African Americans.

In 1955, a woman named Rosa Parks refused to give up her seat on a bus to a white man. At the time, the buses had separate sections for black and white people. Parks had sat in the section for black people. When more white people boarded the bus, she was told to give up her seat for them. She refused and was arrested. King was selected to help lead a boycott against city buses. The boycott lasted 382 days. During the boycott, King's home was bombed, he was arrested, and there were attacks on his church. But he did not give up. The boycott was successful, and black people now had the right to sit where they wanted on the bus. This event made it clear that more work was needed to make sure that everyone had the same civil rights.

King began giving speeches and writing articles. One of his most famous speeches was his "I Have a Dream" speech in Washington, DC. He spoke about how he dreamed of a world in which people would not be judged by their race or color but by their accomplishments.

Unfortunately, King's life was cut short. On April 4, 1968, he was shot while standing on a balcony in Memphis, Tennessee. Today, he is still remembered for his hard work and how he helped change our country.

Answer the questions.

1. When do we celebrate Martin Luther King Jr. Day?

_____

2. On what day was Martin Luther King Jr. born?

_____

3. How old was King when he entered college?

_____

4. What is the name of the organization King joined?

_____

5. Who was the woman who refused to give up her seat on the bus?

_____

6. What did King help lead?

_____

7. What was the name of King's famous speech?

_____

8. Where did King's famous speech take place?

_____

9. Where was King standing when he was shot?

_____

10. What is King remembered for?

_____

Underground Energy

Have you ever seen a volcano spewing hot lava? Maybe you've seen a geyser shooting streams of water. The heat from the lava and the water come from a source within the earth called geothermal energy. But how is such energy possible? Let's take a look.

There are many ways to create energy. Energy can come from wind, water, and even heat. Geothermal energy comes from heat located underground. The word *geo* means "earth" in Greek. The word *thermal* means "heat."

Ten feet (3 m) beneath Earth's surface, the temperature stays between 50 and 60 degrees F (10 to 15.5 degrees C). We can use this resource in the soil to control the temperature in our homes and buildings. To access the energy, holes must be drilled deep underground. Pipes are then buried in the earth. A pumping system pumps the steam or heated water to the surface. Then the heat can be used to keep us warm. The process can also work in reverse. This means it can cool your home during the summer months. The system absorbs the heat in your home, pulling it back into the earth.

Geothermal energy can also be used to make electricity. First, a location for a power plant has to be found. Scientists will look for places where geothermal energy is close to the surface of Earth. One area that is very active is called the Ring of Fire. It can be found around the edge of the Pacific Ocean. In the United States, most geothermal plants are located in the west. This is because hot reservoirs can be found here. Once the plant is built, it taps into the underground reservoirs. The heat from the reservoirs is used to power electrical generators. The biggest plant in the world is located in northern California. It is called The Geysers.

Besides providing heat for your home, geothermal energy can be used in greenhouses to help plants grow, to heat water on fish farms, and even to pasteurize milk.

People like using geothermal energy because it is better for the environment than other types of energy sources. It is also considered a clean energy because it doesn't give off toxins in the air around us. Finally, geothermal energy is efficient. None of it is wasted, so heating bills stay low in winter.

Circle the correct word in parenthesis to complete each sentence.

1. The word *geo* means _____ **("earth"/"heat")** in Greek.

2. _____ **(Ten/Fifty)** feet below the earth's surface, the temperature stays between 50 and 60 degrees F.

3. To access the energy, _____ **(holes/tanks)** must be drilled underground.

4. A pumping system pumps the steam or heated water to the _____ **(sun/surface)**.

5. Geothermal energy can _____ **(cool/heat)** your home in the summer.

6. The Ring of Fire can be found near the _____ **(Pacific/Atlantic)** Ocean.

7. In the United States, most geothermal plants are located in the _____ **(west/east)**.

8. Geothermal energy can be used in _____ **(airplanes/greenhouses)**.

9. People like to use geothermal heat because it is _____ **(renewable/nonrenewable)**.

10. Geothermal heat is considered a _____ **(clean/dirty)** energy.

How to Play Kickball

Getting fresh air and plenty of exercise and increasing your heart rate are good for your health. They can also be tons of fun. Sports like kickball get you outside and increase your energy. Gather a group of friends together and play!

You will need at least six people for each team. Divide your friends into two teams. One way to do this is to pick a team captain. The captains take turns choosing players. You can also ask an adult to choose the players.

Get all your equipment. You will need a big rubber ball and four bases. If you don't have bases, you can improvise. Use sticks, tin cans, or draw your bases with chalk.

Next, position the defensive team on the field. There is an infield and an outfield. The infielders stand near the bases. Their job is to catch the ball and get the player from the offensive team out. The outfielders stand outside of the infield. Their job is to catch the ball when the ball is kicked into the outfield.

Now it's time to play! A pitcher from the team on the field rolls the ball to the kicker. The kicker kicks the ball as hard as possible and runs to first base. The kicker tries to get to the base before a player from the other team catches the ball.

There are many ways for a kicker to be forced out. If the base player catches the ball and touches the base before the kicker gets to the base, the kicker is out. If a player from the other team catches the ball in the air, the kicker is out. If a player from the other team touches the kicker with the ball before the kicker touches the base, the kicker is also out. The kicker can run to the next base if the ball thrown at him or her misses completely.

It is now the next kicker's turn. After kicking the ball, the new kicker runs to first base, and the kicker (now called the runner) on first base runs to second. Every time a kicker/runner runs around all the bases and gets to home plate, the team scores a point. After three outs, however, it's time to switch places.

Play until it's time to go home or back to school. The team with the most points wins!

Use the words from the word bank to label the picture.

infielder   outfielder   first base   kicker   ball

pitcher   home plate   offensive team   defensive team   field

7. _____

8. _____

9. _____

10. _____

6. _____

5. _____

4. _____

3. _____

2. _____

1. _____

The Starry Night

Swirling clouds, curvy mountains, and dark skies sound like a very frightening scene. Don't worry! It's just the description of *The Starry Night*, one of the most famous paintings ever created.

Vincent van Gogh was a Dutch artist born in 1853. He is considered a post-impressionist painter. Post-impressionists used bright colors and thick brushstrokes. They also tended to use geometric shapes and real-life subjects.

In 1888, while living in France, van Gogh had a fight with a fellow painter named Paul Gauguin. Van Gogh was so upset that he went home and cut off his own ear! Many people thought he was crazy. He was placed in a mental health ward at the hospital to help him get better. A year later, while still in the hospital, he painted *The Starry Night*. It is believed that the view from his room was the inspiration for his painting.

This painting was different from all his others. He said that he wanted this painting to be about "the study of night." At the time, it was much more popular to paint scenes of flowers and fields. Van Gogh's heavy brushstrokes and bright colors were different from the type of art that was popular at the time.

Many art critics did not like the painting. They thought it was sloppy and couldn't compare to the more realistic paintings done by other artists. Van Gogh did not get much recognition for his work. He sold only one painting during his entire life. He died a poor man in 1890.

It was only after van Gogh died that people began to see what a great artist he was. Today, his paintings are worth millions of dollars. Van Gogh didn't just paint what he saw in front of him. He painted what he felt in his heart. Some art critics feel that the large strokes and thick lines may represent his struggles. Others say that the bright lights shining down over the dark landscape represent hope. Still others think there might be a hidden religious meaning to the painting. This is what makes art so wonderful. Everyone can decide for him- or herself what the painting means. Take a look at the painting and you decide.

Read each statement. Write *fact* or *inference*.

1. Van Gogh was a Dutch artist. _____

2. He was a post-impressionist painter. _____

3. He had a fight with a painter named Paul Gauguin. _____

4. Van Gogh wanted to try a new way of painting. _____

5. Van Gogh's paintings were not popular during his lifetime. _____

6. Van Gogh did not feel appreciated for his work. _____

7. Van Gogh painted *The Starry Night* while in France. _____

8. Art critics did not like *The Starry Night*. _____

9. Van Gogh was not able to make a living from his painting. _____

10. After he died people began to see what a great artist he was. _____

An Important Man

Benjamin Franklin was one of the most famous people to ever live. He was a writer, an inventor, and a founding father of the United States.

Franklin was born on January 17, 1706, in Boston. He had sixteen brothers and sisters. When he turned twelve, he became an apprentice at his brother's print shop. There, he learned about printing and writing articles. When he turned twenty-three, he bought his own print shop in Pennsylvania. It was called the *Pennsylvania Gazette*.

At the age of twenty-four, Franklin married a woman named Deborah Rogers. Together, they had three children. Unfortunately, one of the children died at the age of four. After he married, Franklin continued to be active in his community. He founded a volunteer fire company and became the postmaster of Philadelphia. He was also a big believer in education, helping to establish Pennsylvania's first university.

Franklin became very interested in inventing items that would make life easier for others. He invented bifocal glasses. These are eyeglasses that allow you to see objects both far away and close up. He also invented the lightning rod. He even invented the Franklin stove, which helped people heat their homes. His most famous discovery involved finding out more about how electricity works. He reportedly did this by using a light, a key, and a string during a lightning storm.

Soon, Franklin became interested in politics. He believed the American colonists should be free from British rule. In the years leading up to the Revolutionary War, he traveled to Britain as a representative of Pennsylvania. In 1775, he was elected to the Continental Congress. As a member of the Continental Congress, he helped create the Declaration of Independence. This made him one of the founding fathers of the new nation.

In 1787, Franklin attended the Constitutional Convention. Here, Franklin helped draft the US Constitution. He was very well respected, so other delegates listened to what he had to say. Once the nation gained independence, Franklin took up a new cause. He was one of the first men to protest slavery. This is because he felt strongly that all men should be free.

When Franklin died in 1790 at the age of eighty-four, more than 20,000 people attended his funeral.

Answer the questions.

1. How many brothers and sisters did Benjamin Franklin have?

_____

2. When Franklin turned twelve, whom did he work for?

_____

3. What was Franklin's job at the print shop?

_____

4. What kind of fire company did Franklin found?

_____

5. What was the type of eyeglasses Franklin invented?

_____

6. What did his most famous discovery involve?

_____

7. As a member of the Continental Congress, what did Franklin help create?

_____

8. What cause did Franklin feel strongly about?

_____

9. How old was Franklin when he died?

_____

10. How many people attended his funeral?

_____

Lady Liberty

There is a very special lady who stands almost fifteen stories tall on Liberty Island in New York Harbor. She represents freedom and democracy. You may know her as the Statue of Liberty. But did you know that she was built in France?

When the American Civil War ended in 1865, France wanted to show its support. The French people came up with the idea of giving a statue to the United States. A sculptor named Frédéric-Auguste Bartholdi was chosen for the job. He asked Alexandre-Gustave Eiffel to help him. Eiffel would later become famous for building the Eiffel Tower in France.

France and the United States worked together to make the project happen. France would be responsible for the statue. The United States would build the pedestal to hold the statue. Each country would help raise money for the project. When it was done, the statue would be a symbol of the friendship between the two countries.

Bartholdi and Eiffel got to work. They wanted to make sure the statue would stand up to the strong winds in the harbor. Bartholdi used sheets of copper to make the skin. He then modeled the face to look like his mother's face. Eiffel was in charge of the statue's skeleton. This was to be made out of iron and steel. Once the skeleton was built, the copper sheets were placed over it.

When Bartholdi finished building the statue, he took it all apart! He had to. There was no other way to ship it. The statue was packed in 214 crates and shipped to New York City by boat. On July 4, 1884, France gave the United States its birthday gift. Workers then spent four months rebuilding the statue. The whole project from start to finish took twenty-one years! When it was complete, it was the tallest structure in the United States.

The statue holds a torch in her right hand and a tablet in her left hand. The date July 4, 1776 is written on the tablet. This is the day the Declaration of Independence was adopted. Including its base, the statue reaches 305 feet (93 m) into the sky. Its nose is 4.5 feet (1.4 m) tall! Today, visitors to the Statue of Liberty can climb the 354 steps up to the crown and look out one of the twenty-five windows.

Read each question and circle the correct answer.

1. What is the main idea of the text?
    a) to discuss the building of New York Harbor
    b) to explain the history of the Statue of Liberty
    c) the importance of freedom for all countries

2. What does *represents* mean in the first paragraph?
    a) stands for   **b)** needs to be   **c)** not a part of

3. Which type of material was **not** used in the building of the statue?
    a) copper   **b)** iron   **c)** gold

4. What island is the Statue of Liberty built on?
    a) Ellis Island   **b)** Liberty Island   **c)** Manhattan

5. What was the statue a symbol of?
    a) friendship between France and the United States
    b) friendship between Bartholdi and Eiffel
    c) It wasn't a symbol of anything.

6. What is the main idea in paragraph four?
    a) how the statue was built   **b)** how the statue was shipped   **c)** how the workers met

7. Whose face did Bartholdi use as a model for the statue?
    a) his sister's   **b)** no one's   **c)** his mother's

8. How many crates were used to ship the statue?
    a) 100   **b)** 214   **c)** 220

9. What does the statue hold in her right hand?
    a) a torch   **b)** a letter   **c)** a book

10. Why is the date written on the tablet important?
    a) It is the date the Declaration of Independence was signed.
    b) It is the date the statue was delivered to New York.
    c) It is not important.

Food for Thought

Do you ever think about the food you eat? If you want to stay healthy and have a lot of energy you have to eat healthy. That is why First Lady Michelle Obama helped to come up with an idea called MyPlate. This is a plate that shows you how much fruits, vegetables, grains, protein, and dairy you should eat. The goal is to eat a variety of nutritious food each day.

According to MyPlate, fruits and vegetables should take up half your plate. This is because fruits and vegetables give you essential vitamins and minerals that your body needs. The vegetable section is just a little bigger than the fruit section. Fruits and vegetables can be pureed, canned, fresh, or frozen. Pears, plums, raisins, berries, and apples are just a few choices.

Now it's time to choose your vegetables. You can pick dark leafy green vegetables like spinach or kale. Red and orange vegetables like carrots, tomatoes, and peppers are good, too. The more colorful your plate, the better!

On the other side of the plate, the grains section is just a little bigger than the protein section. This is because food experts think you should eat more grains than protein. Grains have a lot of fiber and help you feel full longer. Good grains to try are whole-wheat toast, brown rice, oatmeal, and even popcorn.

Let's pick out some protein to complete the plate. Protein is important because it builds and maintains the tissue in your body. Salmon, chicken, turkey, and beans are good choices.

When you look at the plate you can see there is a little side dish for dairy. This is because dairy has calcium, which helps build strong bones and healthy teeth. Good choices for dairy are low-fat milk, yogurt, and cheese.

To learn more about MyPlate, visit www.ChooseMyPlate.gov. You can use MyPlate to help you plan all your meals. It's important to eat from all the food groups to maintain a balanced diet and stay healthy. You may wonder if you have to eat all that food each time. The answer is no. Instead, try to get a variety of foods at breakfast, lunch, and dinner. If you skip vegetables for breakfast, that's okay. Consider having them as a snack later in the day. Remember, if you eat smart, you'll have the energy you need to play hard!

Complete the chart with information from the reading. Place checks in the boxes to choose the correct food groups.

	Fruits	Vegetables	Proteins	Grains	Dairy
1. cheese stick					
2. salmon					
3. peppers					
4. apples					
5. brown rice					
6. yogurt					
7. oatmeal					
8. kale					
9. raisins					
10. chicken					

The Backbone of America

The Rocky Mountain Range is a series of mountains that connect together to form a long line of peaks. This range runs through the western part of North America. It begins in Canada and stretches through a lot of the United States. It runs through Montana, Wyoming, Idaho, Colorado, New Mexico, and Utah. In total, the range spans 3,000 miles (4,828 km)!

The Rocky Mountains began forming billions of years ago when plates beneath Earth's surface collided and buckled. Today, the highest mountain on the range is Mount Elbert in Colorado. It reaches 14,400 feet (4,389 m) high. If you look at the range from a bird's-eye view, you might see that it looks like a long spine. This is how it got its nickname, the Backbone of America. We can learn a lot about nature by studying this range. In fact, many scientists consider the Rocky Mountains a living laboratory. Are you ready to explore?

As we get started on our hike, the first thing we might notice is the weather. The weather on the range depends on the season. Summers are warm and dry, but thunderstorms are common. In the winter, the Rockies are wet and cold. The higher up you go, the heavier the snow.

Next, we might want to look at what types of rocks make up the range. These are mostly igneous and sedimentary rocks. There are also small amounts of volcanic rock. As we continue we might see deep river canyons and basins. These were formed by erosion from wind and water. Long ago, glaciers carved out valleys and lakes. Lush flora and fauna can be found around the rivers and basins. There are more than 1,000 types of flowering plants. One type of tree that is abundant on the range is called the Douglas fir. As we climb higher, there will be fewer flowering plants. Soon we will see only shrubs.

We might also want to look for different types of animals that inhabit the range. The Rocky Mountains stretch over such a wide geological area that it has a wide variety of animals. Some of these animals, such as the lynx and wolverine, are extremely rare. Others include elk, marmot, moose, mountain lions, and grizzly bears.

You have been a good explorer. Next time you go hiking, see what you can discover on your own.

Read each statement. Write *true* or *false*.

1. A mountain range is a series of mountains that connect together. _____

2. The Rocky Mountain Range runs through South America. _____

3. The nickname for the Rocky Mountain Range is the Backbone of America. _____

4. Summers on the mountain range are freezing cold. _____

5. As you climb higher on the range, there is more snow. _____

6. Igneous and sedimentary rocks are two types of rocks found on the mountain range. _____

7. There are only ten different types of flowering plants on the range. _____

8. Douglas fir is a type of tree that can be found on the mountain range. _____

9. Shrubs are found only at the bottom of the range along the lakes. _____

10. Rare animals like the wolverine and lynx can be spotted on the range. _____

Women's Right to Vote

Did you know that every American citizen over the age of eighteen has the right to vote? This was not always the case. Would you believe there used to be a law in the United States saying that only men could vote? Until the 1900s, women in most countries couldn't vote. This idea dates all the way back to ancient Greece!

The word *suffrage* means "the right to vote." The women's suffrage movement was a long and slow process. Many people felt that when it came to voting, race and gender shouldn't matter. The very first meeting to change voting laws happened in 1848 in Seneca Falls, New York. Almost three hundred people went to that meeting. Elizabeth Cady Stanton and Lucretia Mott led it. They had decided to form a group to promote the rights of women.

In 1869, Susan B. Anthony and Elizabeth Cady Stanton formed the National Woman Suffrage Association. Their goal was to get an amendment passed in Congress that would give women and people of all races voting rights. In 1870, the Fifteenth Amendment was approved. It said that men of all races were allowed to vote, but it left out women. Stanton and Anthony did not give up hope.

In 1890, Susan B. Anthony was still fighting for equal voting rights. She became the leader of the National American Woman Suffrage Association. This group of courageous women tried again to get a new amendment passed. This amendment became known as the Nineteenth Amendment. It said that the right to vote should not be based on gender.

Progress was slow. At first, the federal government refused to pass the new amendment. However, some states began agreeing to the idea anyway. In 1893, Colorado was the first state to give women voting rights. By 1896, women were allowed to vote in Utah and Idaho. Washington State adopted an amendment in 1910. Momentum was building. More and more states began to pass amendments.

In 1916, a new party called the National Woman's Party formed to help with the fight. Women began protesting in Washington, DC. Some even went to jail and started hunger strikes. By 1918, President Woodrow Wilson decided to support the Nineteenth Amendment. He signed it into law on August 26, 1920.

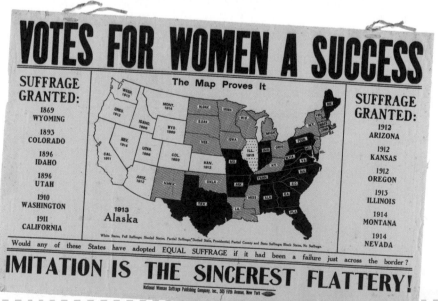

Complete the timeline with the correct year for each statement.

1. _____ The first meeting to change voting laws in Seneca Falls, New York, took place.

2. _____ Susan B. Anthony and Elizabeth Cady Stanton formed the National Women's Suffrage Association.

3. _____ The Fifteenth Amendment was approved.

4. _____ Susan B. Anthony became the leader of the National American Woman Suffrage Association.

5. _____ Colorado gave women the right to vote.

6. _____ Women in Utah and Idaho were allowed to vote.

7. _____ Washington State adopted an amendment to allow women to vote.

8. _____ A new party called the National Woman's Party formed.

9. _____ Woodrow Wilson decided to support the Nineteenth Amendment.

10. _____ The law was signed allowing women the right to vote.

The First Transcontinental Railroad

Did you know that it used to be difficult to get from one end of the country to the other? Today we have airplanes, railroads, and cars. However, in the 1800s people didn't have many choices for travel. Back then, more and more people were heading west to start a new life. The problem was it could take months to get there by covered wagon or boat. It was also hard to transport goods from one part of the country to another.

In 1845, a businessman named Asa Whitney presented an idea to Congress. He wanted to build a railroad that would stretch across the entire country. Many people agreed with Whitney, but Congress was slow to act. In 1861, an engineer named Theodore Judah gathered a group of investors. Together, they formed the Central Pacific Railroad Company. Judah headed to Washington to convince Congress to let his company build the railroad. In 1862, President Abraham Lincoln finally signed the Pacific Railroad Act into law. Construction could now begin on the first transcontinental railroad.

The Central Pacific Railroad would begin building the railroad in Sacramento, California, and continue east. The Union Pacific Railroad would begin building westward from Nebraska. Each railroad would receive money for every mile built. The two railroads would meet somewhere in the middle. The race was on!

Building a railroad was hard work. The workers were made up mostly of Chinese immigrants and Irish laborers. The workers of the Central Pacific Railroad had to face freezing cold winters. Sometimes the only way to get to the other side of a mountain was to blast through it. Then workers would have to build a tunnel. This took a long time. This was because the "iron horse" went right through Native American lands.

On May 10, 1869, the two railroads met at Promontory Summit in Utah. California governor Leland Stanford drove in the final spike. You can still see this spike today. It remains on display at Stanford University in California.

Use the words from the word bank to complete each sentence.

months	California	railroad	west	Nebraska
travel	investors	blast	spike	hard

1. In the 1800s, there were not many choices for _____.

2. It could take _____ to reach the West.

3. Travel became a huge problem as more people moved _____.

4. Asa Whitney's idea was to build a _____ that would stretch across the country.

5. Theodore Judah gathered a group of _____ to form a railroad company.

6. The Central Pacific Railroad would begin building in _____.

7. The Union Pacific began building from _____.

8. Building the railroad was _____ work.

9. Sometimes, the only way to get through a mountain was to _____ through it.

10. Governor Leland Stanford drove the final _____ to complete the railroad.

How Much Do You Know About Magnetic Fields?

Have you ever held two magnets close to one another without allowing them to touch? What does it feel like? They may snap together quickly, or they may try to push apart. The pulling and pushing you feel is known as an invisible magnetic field. Magnets both attract and repel one another. Electric currents create this force.

Every magnet has two ends. One of them is called the north pole, while the other is known as the south pole. There is a saying: "Like poles repel; unlike poles attract." This is because the north pole of one magnet attracts the south pole of another magnet. However, two north poles repel each other. The north pole of all magnets pulls toward the North Pole of Earth. This happens because Earth's core is full of magnetic materials such as molten rocks rich in iron. Earth acts as a giant magnet. Iron is a magnetic material and pulls other magnets toward it. Not all metals are magnetic though. Copper, aluminum, gold, and silver do not attract magnets. Metals that attract magnets are nickel and cobalt. Many alloys are magnetic, too. An alloy is a mixture of metals.

Magnetic fields can cut through all sorts of materials. If you have magnets on your refrigerator holding your artwork, you already know that they can cut through paper. If you place a strong magnet on a chain of unattached paper clips, the magnet will pick up the entire chain and hold them together. This means that magnetic fields can go through metal, too.

It is possible to measure the strength of a magnetic field. The closer you get to the magnet, the stronger its pull. Scientists use units called teslas to measure a magnet's field. Interestingly, Earth's magnetic field is very weak. A small refrigerator magnet has a much stronger magnetic field than Earth's! Next time you find two magnets, test out the magnetic field around them.

Read each statement. Write *true* or *false*.

1. Magnets cannot repel one another. _____

2. Electric currents create a magnet's pulling or pushing force. _____

3. Like poles repel, unlike poles attract. _____

4. Only some magnets have a north pole and a south pole. _____

5. The south pole of all magnets points to Earth's North Pole. _____

6. Magnetic materials such as iron can be found in Earth's core. _____

7. Iron is not a magnetic material. _____

8. An alloy is a mixture of metals. _____

9. It is impossible to measure the strength of a magnetic field. _____

10. A refrigerator magnet has a stronger magnetic field than Earth's. _____

William Penn

William Penn was a lawyer and a landowner best known for founding the colony of Pennsylvania. In 1644, William was born into a wealthy and religious family in London, England. He and his family followed the Church of England. At the time, it was illegal to practice any other religion. This meant that anyone who joined another church could be put in jail. Even so, young William was drawn to the Quaker church. When he was twenty-two, he risked his freedom to become a Quaker. Quakers believe that people should have a right to choose how they practice their religion. They are also pacifists. This means they believe in peace and refused to fight in wars.

WILL^M. PENN.

Penn was arrested for becoming a Quaker. His family was upset and kicked him out of their house. Still, he continued practicing his religious beliefs. Eventually, he became known for his religious writings. Even when he was in jail, he continued to write about his beliefs.

Conditions continued to get worse for Quakers in England. Penn came up with an idea. He thought that the Quakers should have their own colony in North America. The king of England agreed and gave Penn a large area of land. At first, this area was called "Sylvania," meaning "woods." Later, it was changed to Pennsylvania.

Penn wanted this new land to be a haven, or safe place. He helped write a new constitution for Pennsylvania. The constitution guaranteed fair taxes, the protection of private property, and freedom to worship.

In 1682, Penn and one hundred Quakers arrived in the new city of Philadelphia. Once there, he made sure that all citizens had the right to education. This meant that people in Pennsylvania were more literate than in any other colony. The word *literate* means "to have the ability to read and write."

Two years later, close to 4,000 people lived in the colony. Penn returned to England. While there, he had money problems and ended up in debtor's prison. When he returned to Pennsylvania fifteen years later, he saw that the colony he had founded was doing well. Unfortunately, he still had a lot of debt and was forced to return to England once again. He died a poor man in 1718. Today, Penn's ideas of freedom of religion, equal rights for an education, and fair government live on in our democracy.

Read each question and circle the correct answer.

1. What is the main idea of the reading?

    a) to describe the life of William Penn

    b) the importance of education for all

    c) the drawbacks of going to jail

2. Which church did Penn want to join?

    a) Church of England   **b)** Baptist   **c)** Quaker

3. What is an antonym for the word *risk*?

    a) fighting   **b)** safety   **c)** hardy

4. What is the definition of a pacifist?

    a) someone who believes in peace

    b) someone who likes to cook

    c) someone who goes to war

5. What was the original name of Penn's colony?

    a) Penn   **b)** Pennsylvania   **c)** Sylvania

6. What is the main topic of paragraph 3?

    a) Penn thought Quakers should have their own colony.

    b) Penn went to prison.   **c)** Penn fell into debt.

7. What is a synonym for the word *haven*?

    a) a scary place   **b)** a safe place   **c)** an unhappy place

8. What is the main topic of paragraph 4?

    a) the Pennsylvania constitution   **b)** taxes   **c)** freedom

9. What is the definition of the word *literate*?

    a) to be able to read and write   **b)** to be able to sleep   **c)** to be able to see

10. Why did Penn go to debtor's prison?

    a) He didn't go.   **b)** He was hungry.   **c)** He had money problems.

Great Civilizations

Did you know that when Spaniards came to America in the sixteenth century, there were already great civilizations living there? These civilizations had beautiful artwork, complex roads, and big buildings. They were the Maya, Aztec, and Inca. The area they lived in is called Mesoamerica. This area spans Central and South America.

The Maya

The Maya civilization began around 400 BC in Central America. The Maya had an organized government ruled by powerful city-states. They built hundreds of cities with complex roads and large stone buildings. They also built pyramids to worship many gods. The Maya are best known for their written language, called hieroglyphics. They were also advanced in math, art, and even astronomy. Maya used raised fields to farm. This made it easier to keep the soil moist. Their main crops were corn, beans, and squash.

The Aztec

The Aztec lived in central Mexico. They ruled this area from 1200 to 1521. The land they lived on was marshy, so they farmed by using rafts. The main vegetables were corn, beans, tomatoes, and squash. Much of their life revolved around religion. They built temples in the shape of pyramids to worship their many gods. The Aztec capital was Tenochtitlan. This city was the center of trade. Each day, thousands of people came to market to trade gold, silver, and copper. They also had a calendar and a counting system. Along with this, they had a strong educational system. The Aztec allowed both boys and girls to go to school. Boys also trained for war. Their civilization ended when the Spanish conquered them in the early 1500s.

The Inca

The Inca ruled part of South America now known as Peru from the year 1200. They had an advanced system of farming called terrace farming. This was a type of farming used on steep mountains. Their main crops were corn, cotton, and potato. They worshipped the sun god and built temples in his honor. The Inca had skilled workers who built big cities made of stone. They had a complex road system and trade was important. The Inca government charged their people taxes to pay for the cities. Besides a strong government, they were advanced in medicine and knew about diseases. Their civilization ended when the Spanish conquered them in the 1530s.

Read each sentence. Check whether the sentence is about the Maya, Aztec, or Inca.

Statement	Maya	Aztec	Inca
1. They had a government ruled by city-states.			
2. They worshipped the sun god.			
3. Their capital was Tenochtitlan.			
4. They practiced terrace farming.			
5. Their crops were corn, cotton, and potato.			
6. They are best known for their written language, called hieroglyphics.			
7. They went to market to trade gold, silver, and copper.			
8. This government charged their people taxes.			
9. They allowed both boys and girls to go to school.			
10. They built pyramids to worship their many gods.			

Let's Make a Sundial

Today, if we want to know the time, we look at a clock or our watch. In colonial times, it wasn't so easy. Back then, clocks were still new and they didn't always tell the correct time. They often had to be calibrated, or adjusted. Farmers worked during the daylight hours and quit when darkness fell. Church bells rang to let farmers know when it was time to go to church. Many colonists also used sundials to tell time. When the sun cast a shadow on the dial, the colonist could tell what time of day it was.

Let's make our own sundial! You will need the following:
- ❏ Large round pot or bucket
- ❏ Scissors
- ❏ Large piece of cardboard
- ❏ Black marker
- ❏ Ruler
- ❏ Compass
- ❏ Wooden dowel (you can use a pencil or other cylindrical-shaped stick)

Step 1: Trace the outline of the pot or bucket on the cardboard with the black marker.

Step 2: Carefully cut out the circle with scissors.

Step 3: Measure the exact center of the circle with the ruler.

Step 4: Place a dot in the center of the circle with the marker.

Step 5: Measure the end of the dowel.

Step 6: Make a hole the size of the dowel in the cardboard. Remember to keep the hole the same size as the dowel. Fit the end of the dowel through the hole so it is standing vertically.

Step 7: Place your sundial outside facing south in a sunny spot. The compass will tell which way south is.

Step 8: Set an alarm clock in the house to go off every hour. When the alarm goes off, go outside and check where the dowel is casting a shadow on your sundial.

Step 9: Using a ruler, draw the exact line of the shadow and write the time in pencil. For example, if it is 1:00, write the number *1* where the shadow has been cast. Do this every hour for twelve hours.

Step 10: Once you have all the numbers written in pencil, you can retrace them with black marker.

Tip: Make sure you put the sundial in the exact same spot each time you use it.

What's the order? Number the steps *1 to 10.*

_____ Use the marker to place a dot in the center of the circle.

_____ Use scissors to carefully cut out the circle.

_____ Measure the end of your dowel.

_____ Draw the exact line of the shadow. Write the time in pencil every hour for twelve hours.

_____ Find the exact center of the circle.

_____ Make a dowel-sized hole in the cardboard and fit the dowel through it so the dowel is standing up.

_____ Use the marker to trace the outline of your pot or bucket on the cardboard.

_____ Place your sundial outside in a sunny spot facing south.

_____ Retrace the pencil-drawn numbers with the marker.

_____ Go outside every hour and check to see where the dowel is casting a shadow on your sundial.

The Emancipation Proclamation

The American Civil War took place from 1861 to 1865. The North and South were fighting over taxation, state rights, and slavery. In the South, plantation owners used slaves to work the land. President Abraham Lincoln was very much against the idea of slavery. He felt that all men and women should be free.

In September 1862, Lincoln declared that if the South did not return to the Union, all southern slaves would be free. At the time, *the Union* was the term used to refer to the United States. None of the Southern states agreed. On January 1, 1863, Lincoln issued the Emancipation Proclamation. It said, all people "shall be then, thenceforward, and forever free." It also gave black soldiers the right to fight for the Union. Thousands of slaves had already escaped the South to fight on the side of the Northerners. Lincoln knew that with the help of the escaped slaves, the North could win the war.

Unfortunately, the Emancipation Proclamation didn't free a single slave. The Emancipation Proclamation was meant only for states that were against the Union. Some of the Northern states that were in the Union had slaves, too. Under the Emancipation Proclamation people in these states didn't have to set their slaves free just yet. Lincoln understood that this was unfair to the slaves in the Northern states. He also knew that he still needed the support of both the border states and the Northern states where slavery still existed. He didn't want these states to leave the Union.

Slave owners in the South still refused to give up their fight and their slaves. Even so, this was a turning point in the war. Now the war was about freedom for all humans. It also meant that countries such as France and England would be more likely to support the North. This is because France and England were against slavery, too.

Over the next two years, more than 180,000 black soldiers joined the Union army. Many of these soldiers contributed to the Union's victory. They also helped make sure that slaves had everlasting freedom. In 1865, the war finally ended, and with it, so did slavery.

Use the words from the word bank to complete each sentence.

Emancipation Proclamation	free	Union	slaves	against
border states	ended	fight	freedom	soldiers

1. In the South, plantation owners used _____ to work the land.

2. On January 1, 1863, President Lincoln issued the _____.

3. The Emancipation Proclamation said all people should be forever _____.

4. The Emancipation Proclamation gave black soldiers the right to fight for the _____.

5. Lincoln knew he needed the support of the _____.

6. Slave owners in the South would not give up their _____ to keep their slaves.

7. The Emancipation Proclamation helped make the war about _____ for all humans.

8. Countries such as France and England were _____ slavery.

9. After the Emancipation Proclamation was signed, more than 180,000 black _____ joined the Union army.

10. In 1865, the Civil War finally _____.

Traveling at the Speed of Light

Do you like the way the sun feels on your face? Sunlight is important because without it, the world would be dark. We wouldn't be able to see very well, plants wouldn't grow, and Earth would be cold. Sunlight is a source of energy for our planet. But what is light and how does it travel?

Light is a type of energy called electromagnetic radiation. This form of energy is made up of tiny particles called photons. Light travels as a wave. Light energy travels faster than anything else in the entire universe. It races through space at a speed of approximately 186,000 miles (299,338 km) per second. The sun is 93 million miles (149,668,992 km) away from Earth, but light reaches us in only eight minutes. That is pretty amazing. Eight minutes may seem like a long time at first, but if it were possible to drive to the sun at 60 miles (96.6 km) per hour, it would take you 177 years to get there.

There are three ways to control light. You can block it, bend it, or reflect it. Light travels in a straight path called a ray. Rays cannot bend on their own. If rays hit a solid object, they will be blocked, and they will cast a shadow. Unlike sound waves, light waves do not need any matter to help carry along their energy. They can travel in a vacuum, or airless space. However, when light hits a surface, the energy from the light can be absorbed, or soaked up.

If light goes through glass or another transparent material, it will bend. This is because the wavelength of the light has changed. Light travels faster through some materials and slower through others. When the speed changes, the light rays change direction. This is called refraction. Refraction can make an object appear closer than it really is. Glass is a material that is used to refract light. This is why it is used to make eyeglasses.

When light is reflected, it changes its path or bounces back. An example of reflection is when light hits a mirror. The moon is another example of light reflected. It shines because it is reflecting the sun's light.

Read each question and circle the correct answer.

1. What does light provide us with?

    a) a source of energy   **b)** a source of rain   **c)** It does not provide us with anything.

2. Light is made up of tiny particles called _____.

    a) neutrons   **b)** photons   **c)** magnets

3. What does light travel as?

    a) a ball   **b)** a sphere   **c)** a wave

4. How far away is the sun from Earth?

    a) 80 million miles away   **b)** 200 million miles away   **c)** 93 million miles away

5. How long does it take for light from the sun to reach Earth?

    a) fifteen minutes   **b)** eight minutes   **c)** two hours

6. How does light travel?

    a) in a straight path   **b)** in circles   **c)** all different ways

7. If light hits an object that it can't pass through, what happens?

    a) It keeps going.   **b)** It will be blocked.   **c)** Nothing happens.

8. What happens when light goes through glass?

    a) It bends.   **b)** It casts a shadow.   **c)** It is blocked.

9. What is a material used to refract light?

    a) cardboard   **b)** stone   **c)** glass

10. What is it called when light hits a mirror?

    a) refraction   **b)** waves   **c)** reflection

...in the Colonies

...1600s, colonists sailed from Europe to settle in America. They started a new life that is very different from the life we live today. Read about how life has changed since colonial times.

Religion

Colonial Times: Religion was the center of community life. People went to a church or meetinghouse and spent the entire day there. They sat on hard wooden benches while they prayed. They followed very strict religious laws.

Today: Many people still attend religious services, but they are usually not all day, except for certain holidays. A lot of people may also go once a week. And the seats are usually much more comfortable. Also, people may attend religious gatherings outside of their town.

Education

Colonial Times: Children attended a small schoolhouse with only a few children. Boys learned Latin and math, and some went onto colleges in England and later, in America. Girls were taught to read, but they were not allowed to go to college. Many girls didn't go to school at all. Most schools taught religion. If you were a boy, you might go to school to learn a trade.

Today: It is the law that all boys and girls go to school. Girls have the same rights as boys to go to college and get an education. In public schools, religion is not taught.

Food

Colonial Times: Many colonists were farmers and had to grow their own food. They relied on manpower and animal power to plow their fields. Farmers who grew wheat, barley, rice, corn, or tobacco had to haul their goods to market to sell them. Goods were sent to other colonies by boat and wagon. It could take a long time for food to get to people in need.

Today: Even though there are still many farms across the country, most people buy their food at a supermarket. We also rely on heavy machinery and large farm equipment to help make farming easier. Now, food is shipped across country in big shipping containers in much less time.

Recreation

Colonial Times: There was a town center often called a common. There was usually a meetinghouse where people gathered. Children played together making up games, and families discussed the news of the day.

Today: People gather at parks where there are slides and organized activities. If people want to talk, they might go to cafes or call or text one another.

Read each statement. Write *true* or *false*.

1. In colonial times, religion wasn't very important. _____

2. People sat on hard wooden benches when they prayed in colonial times. _____

3. Nowadays, many people attend religious services, but not every day for most of the day. _____

4. In the colonies, girls learned Latin. _____

5. Today, girls and boys have the same rights to an education. _____

6. In the colonies, there were heavy machines to help plow the fields. _____

7. During colonial times, people had to haul their goods to market to sell them. _____

8. A town center used to be called a common. _____

9. In colonial times, people did not gather for meetings. _____

10. Today, people go to parks and participate in organized activities. _____

All About Sleep

You work hard all day, so it's important to get the rest you need at night. Scientists believe that sleep is the time when your brain sorts and stores information. While you sleep, your brain replaces important chemicals. It is also a time for your brain to work out problems. You may think your brain is resting while you sleep, but it turns out that it is very busy helping you stay healthy and grow.

As you get older, you need less sleep. Babies sleep about twelve to fifteen hours a day. School-age children sleep around ten hours a night. Adults usually need about seven to eight hours. It is important not to skimp on sleep. If you do, you might notice that you are clumsier. You can become very cranky and have a hard time thinking clearly. A person who goes five nights without sleeping might even start hallucinating. This means the person can actually start seeing or hearing things that aren't real.

When you lack sleep, your immune system becomes weaker. This is because your body is not functioning properly and you are more likely to get sick. Sleep is also when you do most of your growing. Your muscles, bones, and skin repair themselves while you are sleeping.

Every night, your body goes through sleep cycles. The first stage is when you first get into bed and start to doze off. In this stage you can still wake up easily. Stage 2 is a slightly deeper sleep. This is when your muscles start relaxing and your heart begins to beat slower. You also breathe slower during this stage. Stage 3 is a deeper sleep. Your blood pressure drops, and your body doesn't notice how hot or cold it is. It is much harder to wake up during this time. Stage 4 is the deepest sleep. If you wake up suddenly during this stage, you might be confused. After this stage your body experiences REM, or rapid eye movement. Even though you are sleeping, your eyes are moving back and forth quickly. This is the time when you dream. Your heart might beat faster, and your breathing is not regular. These cycles occur every ninety minutes throughout the night.

When you wake up from a good night's sleep you are refreshed and ready to start the day. Sleep tight!

Circle the correct word in parenthesis to complete each sentence.

1. Scientists believe that sleep is when your brain sorts and _____ (buys/stores) information.

2. While you sleep, your brain replaces important _____ (chemicals/blood vessels) in your body.

3. Sleep is a time for your body to work out _____ (problems/stories).

4. If you skimp on sleep, you might be more _____ (clumsy/happy).

5. When you lack sleep, your _____ (immune system/leg) becomes weaker.

6. Stage 3 is a _____ (light/deep) sleep.

7. Stage 4 is the _____ (deepest/lightest) sleep.

8. If you wake up suddenly during stage 4 sleep, you might be _____ (refreshed/confused).

9. During REM sleep your eyes move back and forth _____ (quickly/slowly).

10. Sleep cycles occur every _____ (two hundred/ninety) minutes throughout the night.

Why Do We Celebrate Veterans Day?

Have you ever walked through your neighborhood around November 11? If so, you might notice that many people have a US flag hanging outside their homes. This is because November 11 is Veterans Day. It is a holiday that honors American soldiers who served in the armed forces. The armed forces are also known as the military. People fly their flags to show their patriotism. This is a way for them to say thank you to soldiers for their hard work and dedication. Veterans Day is not to be confused with Memorial Day. Memorial Day is a holiday that remembers soldiers who died while serving in the military.

In 1919, the country celebrated its first Armistice Day. This was the one-year anniversary of the end of World War I. The word *armistice* means "truce." It is an agreement to stop fighting for a period of time. The reason for Armistice Day was to honor the soldiers who primarily fought during World War I. In 1938, Congress made Armistice Day a national holiday. In 1954, President Eisenhower officially changed the name to Veterans Day. This was because he wanted to show appreciation to all veterans who served in all wars, not just World War I.

Every year on Veterans Day, a ceremony is held in Washington, DC. It takes place at Arlington National Cemetery. During the ceremony, a wreath is placed on the Tomb of the Unknown Soldier. This is a monument that honors soldiers who died but were never identified. After the ceremony, there is a parade. Then the president speaks about the sacrifices our soldiers make to keep our country safe.

People around the country also honor veterans on this day. Every year at 11:00 a.m., there is a moment of silence. This is a time to remember those who have served. Many people also go to parades. At some events, veterans are asked to stand while the audience applauds them for their service. Most schools and official government buildings are closed on Veterans Day.

Today, there are almost 22 million veterans in the United States. You don't have to wait until November 11 to show them your appreciation. The next time you see a veteran, you might consider going up to him or her to say "thank you for your hard work."

Draw a line to match the definition to its word.

1. To give something up to help others   armed forces

2. A show of thanks   identify

3. Someone who once served in the military   ceremony

4. A show of support for one's country, sometimes by waving a flag   monument

5. Commitment to a goal   appreciation

6. An object or statue made to honor someone   armistice

7. This word means "truce"   veteran

8. An event to honor someone   dedication

9. To find out who or what something is   sacrifice

10. Another name for the military   patriotism

All About Germs

Our bodies work hard to keep us healthy. Our heart pumps blood and oxygen. Our stomach helps us digest food. Our brain sends signals to the rest of our body to help us move and think. But sometimes, no matter how hard we try to stay healthy, we still get sick.

Germs live everywhere. They are super small living things called organisms that invade our body. Germs are so tiny that you can only see them through a microscope. There are four different types of germs.

Bacteria are one-celled organisms that can live either inside or outside of the body. Bacteria cause infections. If you have an ear infection or strep throat, bacteria has probably invaded your body. Not all bacteria are bad though. Good bacteria live in our intestines and help us digest the food we eat.

Viruses thrive inside our body. They need a host to survive. However, viruses can be spread from person to person. This is because they need living cells to grow. Once a virus is inside your body, it can spread and make you sick. The flu is a very common virus. A virus can live on surfaces outside the body for a short time, where another person can pick it up and get sick.

Fungi can be singular or multicelled organisms. They like to live in damp places. Most fungi are not harmful to a person who is healthy. They may cause an itchy rash. Sometimes, if a person has sweaty feet, they might get a rash between their toes called athlete's foot.

Protozoa are another type of germ. They live in water. They can cause infections in your intestines. This can give you belly aches and make you feel nauseous.

Once germs get inside our body, they like to stay a long time. They eat up a lot of our energy and some produce toxins. Toxins are proteins that act like poison. The toxins are what make us feel bad. They can cause coughing, aches, and pain.

Most germs spread through air, sweat, saliva, and blood. But there are ways to keep from getting sick. Germs do not like soap and water, so be sure to wash your hands. When you cough or sneeze, cover your mouth and nose. Getting a lot of sleep is also important. Luckily, doctors can often tell us what the germs are doing and how to start feeling better.

Read the sentences. Write whether each is talking about a *bacteria*, *virus*, *fungi*, or *protozoa*.

1. A one-celled organism that can live inside or outside your body. _____

2. This type of germ lives in water. _____

3. This type of germ might appear as a rash on your feet. _____

4. This type of germ can only live outside your body for a short time. _____

5. This can give you belly aches and make you feel nauseous. _____

6. This type of germ needs a host to survive. _____

7. This causes infections. _____

8. The flu is caused by this. _____

9. This type of germ likes to live in damp places. _____

10. Not all of these types of germs are bad. Some live in

    our intestines and help us digest food. _____

The Invention of Machines

Today, we have machines to help us in our daily life. We have cars that help us get around, tractors to help farmers plow, and computers that help us work faster. But have you ever wondered what people did before the invention of machines?

Until the mid-1700s, the United States was an agricultural society. Most people lived in the countryside. They made their living by farming. Any products they needed had to be made by hand. This took a lot of hard work. It also meant that products for sale could only be made in small amounts. But then something changed. People began hearing about the invention of new machines in big cities. These machines ran mostly on steam or coal, and they made work go much quicker. As news of these new inventions spread, people began to move away from the countryside. They headed to the cities to work in factories. The United States began seeing growth in production like never before. This time in history became known as the Industrial Revolution.

The birthplace of the Industrial Revolution was England. Soon, people all across Europe became interested in this new way of life. By the 1800s, news of these big machines spread to the United States. People wanted products that would make their life easier. This meant that businessmen had to find ways to make items quicker and cheaper. It was a time of great innovation and new ideas. The steam locomotive was invented, spinning machines made cloth much quicker than could be done by hand, and iron became easier to produce.

The invention of the railroad changed transportation. No longer did people have to rely on horse and carriage or slow-moving boats to haul their goods. Banking became a big industry, too, as more and more people invested in business. With the invention of the telegraph, communication became easier than ever.

While the Industrial Revolution brought about many positive changes, there was also a downside. Many people were forced to work under poor conditions with little pay. Often, they lived together in cramped and dirty quarters. Life was hard for many people.

Once the Industrial Revolution began, there was no stopping it. Over the years, more machinery was invented to help people in their everyday lives. By the early twentieth century, America was considered the number-one leader of industry.

Answer the questions.

1. Until the mid-1700s, what type of society was the United States?

_____

2. How did most people make a living before the mid-1700s?

_____

3. When machines were first invented what did they mostly run on?

_____

4. As news of inventions spread, where did people begin to move?

_____

5. What was the time in history called when new inventions were being made?

_____

6. What was the birthplace of the Industrial Revolution?

_____

7. What did the invention of the railroad help change?

_____

8. What were more and more people investing in?

_____

9. What invention made communication easier than ever?

_____

10. What kind of conditions were many people forced to work under during the Industrial Revolution?

_____

Becoming a Zoologist

Do you like animals? Maybe when you grow up you'd like to get a job working with them. Scientists who study animals are called zoologists. It is their job to find out more about animal habitats and behavior. They study ways animals are alike or different. They also study the ways animals interact with one another.

There are so many animals in the world that it would be impossible to study them all at once. This is why people who become zoologists choose a specialty. They may want to study an animal as small as an amoeba or as big as an elephant. A zoologist who studies reptiles is called a herpetologist. One who studies mammals is called a mammalogist. A zoologist who studies birds is called an ornithologist.

Some zoologists work at zoos. Others may work in the wild observing animals. This is called field study. Field study is important because it allows zoologists to see how animals live in their natural habitat. Still others hardly work outside at all. Many zoologists work in laboratories. These zoologists study specimens under microscopes. They also conduct experiments. Some zoologists are professors. They work in colleges teaching others about animal behavior.

Zoologists need a certain set of skills to be successful. They must to be able to see even the smallest changes in an animal's behavior. This means the job requires a lot of patience. The ability to problem solve helps them make decisions about how to care for animals and to work well with others. This is because many times zoologists work on teams to get their jobs done. Zoologists usually feel comfortable communicating because they have to give speeches about their findings. They also have to be good writers. They do a lot of research and write articles about their observations.

If you are interested in becoming a zoologist, you can start now. You might want to volunteer at an animal shelter. Sometimes zoos and parks have programs that young people can join to learn more about animals. You may even want to visit a zoologist to ask questions about the job. When you are older, you can take science classes that specialize in the study of animals.

Read each statement. Write *true* or *false*.

1. Zoologists study the ways animals are alike or different. _____

2. There are zoologists who study only certain types of animals. _____

3. A zoologist who studies reptiles is called a herpetologist. _____

4. Field study allows zoologists to observe animals
   in their natural habitat. _____

5. Zoologists do not work in labs. _____

6. Zoologists don't conduct experiments. _____

7. Zoologists must be good at problem solving. _____

8. Being a good writer is an important part of the job. _____

9. Zoologists never have to give speeches. _____

10. Volunteering at an animal shelter is a good
    way to start studying animal behavior. _____

Make Your Own Fossil

Fossils are the remains of plants or animals that have been preserved in stone. For something to be considered a fossil, it has to be more than 10,000 years old. There are two different kinds of fossils: body fossils and trace fossils. Body fossils are evidence of a plant or animal's body found in stones. Trace fossils are the remains of an animal's activity. This could be a footprint, a nest, or even an eggshell.

When an animal or plant dies, it may fall into mud. Over time, the mud hardens and the body or plant dissolves. As the body or plant rots, minerals and groundwater fill its place. Once this hardens it forms a cast. The cast then solidifies in the shape of the animal or plant that has died.

Let's do an experiment. We are going to make our own fossil. You will need glue and modeling clay. You will also need something to make your fossil; this could be a seashell, a small twig, or a small bone. Cover your work surface with newspaper or scrap paper.

Step 1: Place your items on a flat surface.

Step 2: Flatten out your clay, to a 1-inch (2.5-cm) thickness.

Step 3: Choose the object that you want to press into the clay for your fossil. Press firmly, but not too deeply.

Step 4: Carefully take the object out of the clay. Be careful not to push in the edges around your impression.

Step 5: Check to make sure the object left a clear impression. This is called a mold.

Step 6: Now, you are ready to make your casting. Fill in the mold with the white glue. (The glue acts like the minerals and groundwater of a real fossil.)

Step 7: Let the glue dry. This might take a while depending on how deep the mold is. Be sure the glue is completely dry before moving to the next step.

Step 8: Once you are sure the glue is dry, carefully peel away the clay.

Step 9: Peel or cut away any extra glue from your casting.

Step 10: Note your observations. Does your casting look like the original object? What is the same? What is different?

What's the order? Number the steps *1* to *10*.

_____ Peel or cut away any extra glue from your casting.

_____ Note your observations.

_____ Once you are sure the glue is dry, carefully peel away the clay.

_____ Press the object you chose firmly into the clay.

_____ Check to make sure the object left a clear impression.

_____ Place your items on a flat surface.

_____ Flatten out your clay, to a 1-inch (2.5-cm) thickness.

_____ Fill in the mold with the white glue.

_____ Carefully take the object out of the clay.

_____ Let the glue dry completely.

Anne Hutchinson and Religious Freedom

Today, people in our country have the right to practice their religious beliefs and live the way they choose. This was not always the case, especially for women. Anne Hutchinson helped to change that.

Hutchinson was born in England in 1591. Her father was a deacon for the Church of England. He taught Anne to think for herself and to stand up for her beliefs. When she was older, she married a man named William Hutchinson. Together, they joined a Protestant church. The head of this church was a Puritan minister named John Cotton. Puritans wanted to bring purity back to the church. They felt that religion had become corrupt, or dishonest. King James I of England did not like the Puritans. He felt threatened by them. Because of this, a group of Puritans decided to move to the colonies. Here, they established the Massachusetts Bay Colony as their new home.

Hutchinson was hopeful that she would be able to practice her beliefs the way she thought best in the New World. She was wrong. She did not agree with all the Puritan rules, and she refused to follow them. She thought that her faith was enough to please God. But the Puritans were very strict and were not happy with Hutchinson's decision to do what she wanted.

Hutchinson was very smart and strong willed. She believed that everyone had the right to make personal decisions. She thought that women were just as capable as men to learn and pray. Soon, she began to gather women to study religion and read the Bible. She preached that being a good person was very important. These meetings became very popular. This concerned the Puritan leaders, because they thought that she was ruining the Puritan community.

Eventually, Hutchinson was arrested and put on trial. She was banned from the colony, so she moved to Rhode Island with her husband and children. Later, she moved to New York. In 1643, Native Americans killed her when they raided her home.

Hutchinson is remembered for being outspoken and standing up for her beliefs. She is considered a symbol of tolerance and religious freedom. If you go to the Massachusetts State House, you will find a statue there standing in her honor.

Read each question and circle the correct answer.

1. Where was Anne Hutchinson born?

   a) Paris   **b) England**   c) New York

2. What was Hutchinson's father?

   a) a deacon   b) a doctor   c) a lawyer

3. What was Hutchinson's husband's name?

   a) Tom   b) Fred   **c) William**

4. What church did Hutchinson and her husband join?

   a) Protestant   b) Catholic   c) Baptist

5. Which religious group did Hutchinson become a part of?

   a) Quakers   **b) Puritans**   c) Pilgrims

6. What did Hutchinson hope to practice freely in the New World?

   a) her religion   b) her music   c) her medicine

7. What were the Puritans considered?

   a) strict   b) easygoing   c) serious

8. Who came to Hutchinson's meetings to read and study the Bible?

   a) men   **b) women**   c) nobody

9. What did the Puritan leaders do to Hutchinson?

   a) helped her   b) left her alone   **c) arrested her**

10. Today, what is Hutchinson considered a symbol of?

   a) hope   **b) tolerance**   c) love

How Sand Dunes Form

Erosion of Earth's surface happens when materials break down and are carried away. Wind is a natural weathering agent that can cause this. The best place to see how wind erodes Earth's surface is in the desert or on the beach. This is where sand dunes occur. In these places, wind carries sand an inch or two (2.4–5.1 cm) above the ground until it hits an obstacle such as a rock or a tree. Because the sand cannot continue on its journey, it begins to accumulate.

Sand dunes have two sides. They are the windward side and the slip-face side. The windward side is the side that the wind hits. It is also the side that continuously pushes the sand up. The windward side has a rough surface. The slip-face side is smoother. This is the side away from the wind.

As the wind blows, it continues to move the sand up to the top of the dune. The stronger the wind blows the sand, the taller the dune. Eventually, the dune becomes too steep and begins to collapse from the weight of the sand. The sand begins to slide down the slip face. It stops falling when a steep angle is formed. This process stabilizes the dune. The angle that is formed is called the angle of repose.

In some places, you can find a series of dunes. This is known as a dune belt. A field full of dunes is called erg. Dunes that form underwater are called subaqueous dunes. They are built up by strong currents and can be found in oceans and rivers.

Very limited animal and plant life can survive living in a sand dune. There is hardly any soil, so plants with deep root systems cannot survive. Often, sand dunes that are located on beaches grow a type of grass called beach grass. This grass can tolerate salty air.

Sand dunes are constantly changing, making the sand unstable. Most animals cannot find homes in an unstable environment. However, there are certain animals that can live in sand dunes. One of them is called a sandfish. A sandfish is actually a lizard that can swim through the sand.

The next time you are at the beach, look for sand dunes. See if you can identify some of their features.

Use the words from the word bank to complete each sentence.

erosion	erg	rough	smooth	taller
collapse	subaqueous	sandfish	obstacle	beach grass

1. _____ happens when materials from Earth's surface break down and are carried away.

2. Wind carries sand an inch or two (2.4–5.1 cm) above the ground until it hits an _____.

3. The windward side has a _____ surface.

4. The slip-face side has a _____ surface.

5. The stronger the wind, the _____ the dune.

6. When the dune becomes too steep, it begins to _____.

7. Dunes that form underwater are called _____.

8. A field full of dunes is known as an _____.

9. Dunes on the beach grow a type of grass called _____.

10. A _____ is a lizard that can swim through the sand.

The Abolitionist Movement

Beginning in the 1600s, slavery in America had become a way of life. Africans were brought on ships from the African continent and sold to landowners. The slaves had no rights and had to work under poor conditions. Many landowners felt that they needed to have enslaved people to work the land. This was especially true in the South, where big plantations produced cotton, sugarcane, rice, and tobacco.

By the 1700s, people slowly began to protest slavery. Many people thought that all men should be free. In the North, there was less need for slaves. Many people lived in big industrial cities and didn't depend on their land for profit as much as the people in the South.

By 1810, the Underground Railroad was formed. This was a way to help enslaved people escape from their owners and find freedom. People along the route of the Underground Railroad hid slaves and helped them until they found their way to safety.

In 1831, the Abolitionist Movement formed in the North. This was a group of people that came together to fight for the emancipation of enslaved people. The word *emancipation* means "to be set free."

In the meantime, people continued to protest. The protesters wanted to make other people aware of why slavery was so bad. They began writing newspaper articles and handing out pamphlets explaining why slavery should be abolished. One famous writer was Frederick Douglass, who had escaped from slavery. He became a leader in the Abolitionist Movement. Other people went straight to the government. They asked their representatives to support their cause. Sometimes the protests were violent. In 1859, there was a raid at a place called Harpers Ferry in Virginia. A man named John Brown led twenty-one men into an armory to steal weapons. They planned to cause an uprising and fight for the freedom of enslaved people. Brown was arrested and hanged for treason. Treason is when someone rebels against the government.

It took many years for slavery to be abolished. In 1861, the Civil War broke out between the North and South. Part of the reason for the war was to end slavery. When the war was over in 1865, the Thirteenth Amendment was added to the Constitution. This amendment freed all enslaved people in the United States.

Answer the questions.

1. What four items did Southern plantations grow?

_____

2. By the 1700s, what were people protesting?

_____

3. Why was there less need for enslaved people in the North?

_____

4. In 1831, what movement formed in the North?

_____

5. What does the word *emancipation* mean?

_____

6. What was the purpose of the Underground Railroad?

_____

7. What was the name of the famous leader of the Abolitionist Movement who escaped from slavery?

_____

8. Who led the raid at Harpers Ferry?

_____

9. What was John Brown charged with?

_____

10. What was the amendment that ended slavery?

_____

Let's Volley

Volleyball is a popular sport. It can be played in a park, on a beach, or in a gymnasium. A man named William Morgan invented the game in 1895. Morgan was a teacher who lived in Massachusetts. He took his ideas from tennis, baseball, and handball. Morgan started out by taking a tennis net and raising it 6.5 feet (1.98 m) into the air. He even had nine innings, just like in baseball. Today, the rules have evolved. This means they are much different than they used to be.

The goal of the game is to send the ball over the net so that the other team cannot return the ball. You will need two teams of six players each. Each team stands on one side of the court in one to three rows.

First, you choose a server to hit the ball over the net to the opposite team. The server stands in the back right corner. The server throws the ball in the air with one hand and tries to hit it over the net with the other hand.

Then, the other team tries to return the ball without allowing it to hit the ground. The team has three hits to get it over the net. You can hit the ball with any part of your body.

Each team continues to volley the ball back and forth over the net until the ball hits the ground. The team that scores gets to serve the next ball. This is a good time to rotate players. The first team to score 25 points wins, but you can choose to play for fewer points.

There are many ways to score. The other team scores a point:

if the ball hits the ground on your side of the net
if someone touches the net
if someone's foot goes under the net
if a teammate hits a ball twice in a row
if your team hits the ball more than three times

Volleyball is a great game. It requires teamwork and builds communication. It also helps improve balance and flexibility. Now, let's volley!

Read each statement. Write *true* or *false*.

1. The game of volleyball was invented in 1990. _____

2. William Morgan invented the game. _____

3. Morgan was a doctor. _____

4. Morgan placed the volleyball net 6.5 feet (1.98 m) in the air. _____

5. The goal of the game is to send the ball over the net. _____

6. There are three players on each team. _____

7. The server stands in the back left corner. _____

8. The other team scores a point if the ball hits the ground
   on your side of the net. _____

9. A team can hit the ball up to five times before
   hitting it over the net and still score. _____

10. Volleyball helps improve flexibility. _____

The Branches of Government

The Constitution of the United States was written in 1787. It is a set of the highest rules and laws in the country. It also explains how our nation should be governed. When the leaders of the states got together to write the Constitution, they intended for the laws to be fair. They wanted to protect the rights of people. They also wanted to make sure that the government would not be able to abuse its power. The leaders decided that a good way to do this was to have three branches of government. This way, each branch could check on the other. This is a checks-and-balances system. The three branches of government are the executive branch, the legislative branch, and the judicial branch.

The Executive Branch

The president of the United States is the head of this branch of government. It is the president's job to direct the government and recommend new laws. He or she also approves laws that the legislative branch passes. It is the president's right to veto any laws that he or she doesn't think are good for our country. The president has many other duties, too. He or she is the commander-in-chief of the armed forces, and negotiates treaties with other countries.

The Legislative Branch

This branch of government is made up of the two houses of Congress. They are the Senate and the House of Representatives. It is their job to make the laws. They can also impeach other members of government and approve treaties. There are 100 senators in Congress, two for each state. There are 435 representatives in the House. The larger a state's population, the more representatives it has in Congress.

The Judicial Branch

This branch is in charge of the court system. The Supreme Court heads this branch of government. It is the judicial branch's job to interpret the meaning of the Constitution and the laws that Congress has passed. This is done through court cases. The Supreme Court is different from criminal courts. It only decides if an act is unconstitutional or constitutional. There are nine judges on the Supreme Court.

Read each sentence. Check whether the sentence is about the executive, legislative, or judicial branch.

Statement	Executive	Legislative	Judicial
1. The president is the head of this branch.			
2. This branch is made up of two houses.			
3. This branch is in charge of the court system.			
4. This branch is head of the armed forces.			
5. This branch has 100 senators.			
6. This branch decides whether a law is constitutional or unconstitutional.			
7. It is this branch's job to make laws.			
8. This branch negotiates treaties with other countries.			
9. This branch interprets the meaning of the Constitution.			
10. This branch can veto laws.			

Let's Look at the Earth's Layers

Have you ever spent time digging at the beach? Maybe you've wondered what is beneath all that sand. Some scientists compare Earth to an onion. This is because, like an onion, Earth has layers. The layers of Earth are the crust, the mantle, and the core.

Earth's crust is the outer layer where we live. It is made up of mountains, water, and soil. On land, Earth's crust is about 25 miles (40 km) thick. Under the oceans, it is only 3 to 5 miles (4.8 to 8 km) thick. Scientists know more about Earth's crust than about any other layer because we live here, and it is easy to explore.

The mantle is the next layer. It has a thickness of 1,802 miles (2,900 km) and makes up 84 percent of Earth's weight. The mantle is composed of thick, hot semisolid rocks, along with iron and other minerals. Intense heat in the mantle causes the rocks to move. When they cool, they sink down to the next layer, which is Earth's core. Here they crash into one another, causing earthquakes and volcanic eruptions.

Earth's core is made up of two layers. They are the inner core and the outer core. Both are located at the center of Earth. The inner core is solid and dense. It is made up of iron and nickel. This part of Earth is estimated to be about 1,500 miles (2,414 km) thick. The heat of the inner core is between 9,000 and 13,000 degrees F (between 4,982 and 7,204 degrees C). That is incredibly hot! As a matter of fact, it is as hot as the surface of the sun. The metal doesn't melt because of the pressure around the inner core.

The temperature of the outer core is between 7,200 and 9,000 degrees F (between 3,982 and 4,982 degrees C). This part of Earth is not under as much pressure as the inner core. This means that the iron and nickel have a chance to melt. The movement of these liquid metals, known as molten lava, creates Earth's magnetic field. The magnetic field is a protective barrier around Earth that keeps us safe from the sun's solar wind. The outer core is 1,430 miles (2,301 km) thick.

It is not easy to explore the inner layers of Earth. One reason is because as we get closer to the core, it becomes way too hot. Instead, scientists use a machine called a seismograph to measure energy waves that travel through Earth.

Circle the correct word in parenthesis to complete each sentence.

1. Scientists compare Earth's layers to that of an _____ **(onion/apple)**.

2. The crust is the _____ **(inner/outer)** layer of Earth.

3. Scientists know more about the _____ **(crust/core)** than about any other layer.

4. The mantle makes up _____ **(10 percent/84 percent)** of Earth's weight.

5. Earth's core is made up of _____ **(five/two)** layers.

6. The inner core is as hot as the surface of the _____ **(moon/sun)**.

7. The core is made up of iron and _____ **(granite/nickel)**.

8. In the outer core, the iron and nickel have a chance to _____ **(solidify/melt)**.

9. The liquid metals in the outer core are known as _____ **(oil/molten lava)**.

10. The magnetic field is a protective barrier around Earth that keeps us safe from the sun's solar _____ **(wind/ice)**.

The Life of Thomas Jefferson, Founding Father

Thomas Jefferson was one of the founding fathers of our nation. He was also a farmer, a lawyer, and a president of the United States.

In 1743, Jefferson was born on a plantation in Virginia. While growing up, he enjoyed riding horses and playing the violin. He went to school and became a lawyer in 1767. He also continued to farm the huge estate that his father had left him in Virginia. In 1768, he began to prepare his land for a brick mansion that he was going to build. This mansion would be called Monticello.

Jefferson eventually began taking an interest in politics. In 1769, he became a member of the Virginia legislature. Not long after, in 1772, Jefferson married a woman named Martha Skelton. Together, they had six children, but four of them died young.

In 1775, the Revolutionary War was well under way, and American colonists were fighting for freedom. Jefferson was selected to be a delegate in the Continental Congress. This was a group of men who came together to create America's new government. Jefferson was known for his good writing skills, so he was asked to draft a copy of the Declaration of Independence. This document explained why the American colonies deserved to be free from British rule. The Declaration was adopted on July 4, 1776.

After helping to create the Declaration of Independence, Jefferson was elected as governor of Virginia in 1779. During the following years, he continued to build his political career. In 1796, Thomas Jefferson decided to run for president of the United States. He lost the election but became vice president. Four years later, he decided to run again. This time he tied with his opponent! Congress had to make the decision. They chose Jefferson, who became the third president of the United States. He was sworn into office on March 4, 1801. He served two terms but decided not to run for a third time.

After his presidency, he moved back to Monticello where he devoted his time to music and gardening. He died on July 4, 1826, when he was eighty-three years old.

Complete the timeline with the correct year for each statement.

1. _____ Jefferson was born on a plantation in Virginia.

2. _____ Jefferson became a lawyer.

3. _____ Jefferson prepared to build his mansion, Monticello.

4. _____ Jefferson became a member of the Virginia legislature.

5. _____ Jefferson married Martha Skelton.

6. _____ The Declaration of Independence was adopted.

7. _____ Jefferson was elected governor of Virginia.

8. _____ Jefferson decided to run for president of the United States but lost the election.

9. _____ Jefferson was elected third president of the United States.

10. _____ Jefferson died at the age of eighty-three.

America's Pioneers

The original thirteen colonies were all located on the east coast of North America. By the late 1700s, the number of people living there had grown. There was a great need for new land and resources. The colonists knew that there was unclaimed land west of the Appalachian Mountains. Many packed up their belongings to settle this untamed territory. These brave people became known as pioneers.

Some pioneers were hunters and trappers, while others were farmers and even miners. All were looking for a new start. Their goal was to head west in a caravan with others. They spent long months traveling in covered wagons and setting up camp along the road. Sometimes more than thirty wagons traveled together. On days when it rained, mud covered the wagon wheels and animals. When the weather was nice, a caravan might be able to travel 20 miles (32 km).

In 1788, pioneers began to settle land that became known as the Northwest Territory. This was an area made up of Indiana, Ohio, Michigan, Wisconsin, and Illinois. Then, in 1803, Thomas Jefferson made an agreement with the French. He purchased the land west of the Mississippi River. Jefferson paid 15 million dollars for the land that became known as the Louisiana Territory. The United States had now doubled in size.

In the years that followed, the United States continued to grow. People believed that it was the country's divine right to expand all the way to the Pacific Ocean. This idea became known as Manifest Destiny. Soon, people were settling into Texas, Oregon, and California.

When pioneers finally reached their new homes, they realized their new life was not going to be easy. They had very little food. This meant they had to hunt for animals and gather berries until they could plant crops. As people pushed into Texas, a war with Mexico broke out over land borders. In other parts of the West, pioneers faced problems with Native American tribes who didn't want to give up their land. Many Native American tribes were eventually forced to live on reservations the US government controlled.

The pioneers faced many hardships as they pushed westward to find new opportunities. Through hard work and determination they were able to build a new life for themselves.

Read each question and circle the correct answer.

1. What is the definition of pioneers?
   a) a group of people who stay in one place
   b) a group of people who are the first to explore new territory
   c) a group of people who like to dance

2. What is the main idea of the second paragraph?
   a) It tells what it was like to travel west.   b) How difficult it was to travel.
   c) The excitement of camping on the road.

3. From whom did Thomas Jefferson buy the Louisiana Territory?
   a) the British   b) the French   c) the colonists

4. What was the area of Ohio, Michigan, Wisconsin, and Illinois called?
   a) Southwest Territory   b) Northwest Territory   c) Eastern Territory

5. What is Manifest Destiny?
   a) the belief that people should live together in peace   b) a document about man
   c) the belief that it was the country's divine right to expand

6. What is the definition of a caravan?
   a) people who travel together in a group
   b) a person traveling by himself
   c) someone who doesn't like to travel

7. When the pioneers reached their new home, what were they lacking?
   a) food   b) water   c) transportation

8. What is the main idea of the fifth paragraph?
   a) the celebrations the pioneers had in their new land
   b) the wars the pioneers fought
   c) the hardships the pioneers faced

9. When the pioneers pushed into Texas, which country did they have a war with?
   a) Mexico   b) France   c) England

10. Where were many Native Americans forced to live once the pioneers took over
    their land?
    a) in huts   b) on reservations   c) on houseboats

The Secrets of the Prairie

The US Great Plains is an area made up of broad, flat land. At first glance, the plains may look dull and boring. If you look closer, it is full of hidden secrets and exciting history.

The Great Plains is sometimes called the prairie. This is because of the wide-open land and the tall grasses that grow there. The land stretches across ten different states, reaching from Texas to Montana and all the way to Canada. Just over to the West, the Rocky Mountains tower over the plains. Some even call the Great Plains the "doormat" of the Rockies.

Grass is the main type of growth on the prairie. In some parts of the Great Plains the grass might grow as high as 12 feet (3.7 m) tall! But the land is very dry. It gets less than 20 inches (0.5 m) of rain per year. This makes it hard for vegetation to grow. The only places you might see trees are along rivers and creeks. Because it is so dry, the area is home to a lot of dust storms. Strong winds whip through the plains, eroding the land and blowing away the topsoil. Sometimes these winds are so strong, they turn into dangerous tornadoes.

For thousands of years, the Great Plains was home to many animals such as prairie dogs, wolves, coyotes, and rattlesnakes. However, the most abundant animals were the wild herds of buffalo that roamed freely. The buffalo was food for many Native American tribes such as the Cheyenne and Sioux. They lived off the land, hunting the buffalo for food and using their hide for clothing and shelter.

In the mid-1800s, pioneers began to settle the area. Like the Native Americans, the settlers hunted the buffalo, too. Only the settlers were not careful. They killed too many too fast, and the buffalo nearly became extinct. Another way farmers changed the landscape was to plow the tall, sweeping prairie grass to grow crops such as wheat.

Today, the Great Plains is made up mostly of large cattle ranches and other farms. Farmers have also found a way to make good use of the wind that blows through the prairie. They have built huge windmills to harness energy. They sell the energy from the windmills to electric companies for electricity.

Use the words from the word bank to complete each sentence.

flat	doormat	rain	shelter	ten
pioneers	cattle	plowed	windmills	buffalo

1. The Great Plains are made up of _____ land.

2. The land stretches across _____ different states.

3. Some call the Great Plains the _____ of the Rockies.

4. The Great Plains gets less than 20 inches of _____ a year.

5. At one time, the most abundant animals were the wild herds of _____.

6. The Native Americans used buffalo hide for clothing and _____.

7. In the mid-1800s, _____ began settling the land.

8. Farmers _____ the tall prairie grass to grow crops.

9. Today, the Great Plains is made up mostly of _____ ranches.

10. Farmers built huge _____ to harness the wind's energy.

Colonial Muffins

In colonial times, corn was an important food staple. When colonists came to America, they found that Native Americans depended on corn for their survival. It was easier to grow than wheat and could be used in a lot of different recipes. Once the farmers harvested the corn, they would dry and store it. When it was ready, they made cornmeal out of it. They did this by pounding the corn or grinding it with a mortar and pestle. Farmers used every part of the corn plant. Nothing was wasted. The stalks and leaves were good for feeding the farm animals. Cornhusks could be used as brooms or to stuff mattresses. Even the cobs were used to help start fires. Let's step back in time and make colonial corn muffins.

You will need:

A 12-cup muffin tin	A large bowl	A large spoon for mixing
Measuring cups	Measuring spoons	

Ingredient List:

Cooking spray	1 egg	3 tablespoons sugar
1 ½ cups milk	2 cups yellow cornmeal	1 tablespoon baking powder
⅓ cup vegetable oil	1 cup all-purpose flour	1 teaspoon salt

With the help of an adult, turn your oven on to 425°F (218°C).

Step 1: Spray your 12-cup muffin tin with cooking spray.

Step 2: Measure 1 ½ cups of milk and pour into your large bowl.

Step 3: Add ⅓ cup of vegetable oil to the bowl.

Step 4: Crack 1 egg and mix with the milk and oil.

Step 5: Measure out 2 cups of yellow cornmeal and add it to the bowl.

Step 6: Add 1 cup of all-purpose flour.

Step 7: Using your measuring spoons, add 3 tablespoons of sugar.

Step 8: Add 1 tablespoon of baking powder.

Step 9: Add 1 teaspoon of salt.

Step 10: Mix all of the ingredients together.

Using your large spoon, carefully pour the batter into the muffin tin. Make sure to leave a little extra room for the muffins to rise. Bake the muffins for 18 minutes or until they turn a golden color. Eat and enjoy!

Answer the questions.

1. What did colonial Americans find harder to grow than corn?

_____

2. Once the farmers harvested corn, what was the first thing they had to do to it?

_____

3. What did colonial Americans use to grind their corn?

_____

4. To make the corn muffin recipe, at what temperature do you have to set the oven?

_____

5. In step 2, how much milk are you supposed to pour into the large bowl?

_____

6. At what step do you add an egg to the bowl?

_____

7. How much baking powder does the recipe call for?

_____

8. For which steps will you need to use your measuring spoons?

_____

9. What does the last step ask you to do?

_____

10. For how long are you supposed to bake the muffins?

_____

The Thirteen Colonies

In the early seventeenth century, people from Great Britain became interested in the Americas. Many were drawn to this land in search of religious freedom. Others came to find new opportunities to work the land and make their fortune in trade. Still others came to seek adventure. Between 1607 and 1732, these people established the thirteen colonies along the Atlantic coast of North America. The colonists brought their families to unknown lands and started a new life together. In many ways, the colonies were similar, but they had their differences, too. Look at the chart to compare how the colonies were the same and how they differed.

Colony Name	Region	Geography	Religion	Trade	Founder
Connecticut	New England	forests, hills, poor soil, long winters	Puritan	farming, shipbuilding, rum	Thomas Hooker
Delaware	Mid-Atlantic	flatlands, rivers, valleys	Quakers, Catholics, Lutherans, Jews	farming, production of iron ore	Peter Minuit
Georgia	Southern	fertile soil, coastal plains, tidewaters	Anglican, Baptist	agriculture, tobacco, sugar	James Oglethorpe
Maryland	Southern	fertile soil, coastal plains, tidewater	Anglicans, Catholics, Baptists	tobacco, sugar	George Calvert
Massachusetts	New England	forests, hills, poor soil, long winters	Puritan	farming, fishing, shipbuilding	John Winthrop
New Hampshire	New England	forests, hills, poor soil, long winters	Puritan	farming	John Mason
New Jersey	Mid-Atlantic	flatlands, hills, valleys	Quakers, Catholics, Lutherans, Jews	farming	Lord Berkeley
New York	Mid-Atlantic	flatlands, hills, valleys	Quakers, Catholics, Lutherans, Jews	farming, production of iron ore	Duke of York
North Carolina	Southern	fertile soil, coastal plains, tidewaters	Anglican, Baptist	tobacco, sugar	a group of colonists
Pennsylvania	Mid-Atlantic	flatlands, hills, valleys	Quakers, Catholics, Lutherans, Jews	wheat, farming, production of iron ore	William Penn
Rhode Island	New England	forests, hills, poor soil, long winters	Puritan	shipbuilding, farming, rum	Roger Williams
South Carolina	Southern	fertile soil, coastal plains, tidewaters	Anglican, Baptist	tobacco, sugar	a group of colonists
Virginia	Southern	fertile soil, coastal plains, tidewaters	Anglican, Baptist	tobacco	John Smith

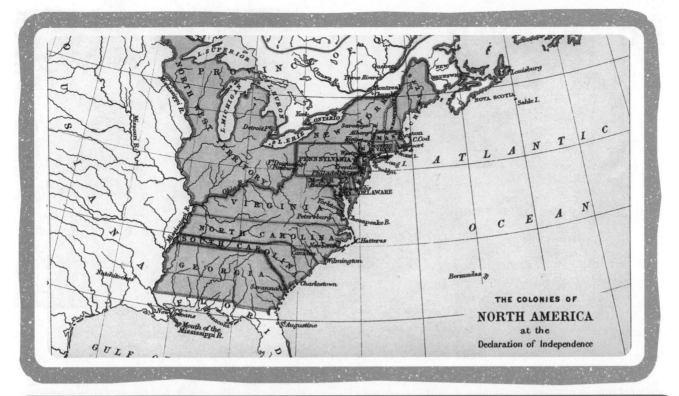

THE COLONIES OF
NORTH AMERICA
at the
Declaration of Independence

Read each statement. Write *true* or *false*.

1. Thomas Hooker was the founder of the Connecticut colony. _____

2. The main type of trade in Delaware was tobacco. _____

3. Baptist was one of the religions practiced
   in the colony of Georgia. _____

4. New Jersey was considered a Mid-Atlantic colony. _____

5. Maryland has poor soil. _____

6. One of the industries in North Carolina was sugar. _____

7. The colony of Rhode Island was located in New England. _____

8. The colony of Pennsylvania had flatlands, hills, and valleys. _____

9. John Smith founded the colony of New York. _____

10. South Carolina was a Mid-Atlantic colony. _____

The Fourth President

James Madison was born in the colony of Virginia in 1751. He grew up on a farm with eleven brothers and sisters. James was very studious, meaning he did well in school. One of his favorite pastimes was reading. When he was old enough, he went to the College of New Jersey. Today, this college is known as Princeton University. James studied so much that he graduated in two years instead of four.

By the time Madison was finished with college, he knew that he wanted a career in politics. He went home to Virginia and was elected to the state legislature. As part of his job, he fought for religious freedom. Madison also wanted to help the colonies gain freedom from British rule. In 1780, he was elected to the Continental Congress. Here, he met Thomas Jefferson. The two quickly became close friends.

In 1787, Madison was asked to attend a meeting called the Constitutional Convention. This was an important meeting in Philadelphia at which the colony leaders gathered to create the rules for a new government. It was at this meeting that the US Constitution was written. It was Madison's job to read the final version of the Constitution to make sure it was correct. He also kept notes about the meeting. Two years later, Madison proposed amendments to the Constitution. These amendments guaranteed the rights and liberties of the people. They became known as the Bill of Rights.

In 1794, Madison married a woman named Dorothea Payne Todd. Dorothea was a widow who had one child. She is known for being very social and hosting lively parties.

In 1808, Madison was elected president of the United States. While he was president, a war broke out between France and Britain. This war was called the War of 1812. At first, Madison did not want to get involved in the war. But then Britain attacked US trade ships. Madison had no choice but to declare war on Britain. The war was hard for our new nation. The British troops won many battles. They even burned down the White House. Eventually, the war turned, and the United States won at the Battle of New Orleans. This made Madison a popular president.

After his presidency, Madison retired to his home in Virginia. He died on June 28, 1836, at the age of eighty-five.

Read each question and circle the correct answer.

1. Where was James Madison born?

   a) Virginia   **b)** New York   **c)** California

2. What does the word *studious* mean?

   a) to spend a lot of time farming   **b)** to spend a lot of time studying

   c) to spend a lot of time riding horses

3. How long did it take James Madison to graduate college?

   a) one year   **b)** five years   **c)** two years

4. As part of his job in the legislature, what did Madison fight for?

   a) religious freedom   **b)** children's rights   **c)** the right to vote

5. What was the name of the meeting Madison was asked to attend in 1787?

   a) the Confederate Meeting   **b)** the Constitutional Convention

   c) the Declaration Meeting

6. What important document was written at the meeting in 1787?

   a) the US Constitution   **b)** the Declaration of Independence   **c)** the Bill of Rights

7. What did the Bill of Rights guarantee?

   a) the right to go to war   **b)** the rights and liberty of the people   **c)** nothing

8. What year was Madison elected president?

   a) 1801   **b)** 1797   **c)** 1808

9. During the War of 1812, what building did Britain burn?

   a) the White House   **b)** the Washington Monument   **c)** the Capitol

10. How old was James Madison when he died?

   a) seventy   **b)** eighty-five   **c)** eighty-two

Water Power

Hydropower comes from the energy created by the force of moving water. The word *hydro* means "water" in Greek. Water is a renewable energy source. This means it can be easily replaced. When the sun heats water in the ocean, the water turns to vapor. The vapor rises into the atmosphere and turns to clouds. When cold air mixes with the clouds, the clouds release water back down to Earth.

The use of hydropower is not new. It dates back all the way to ancient times. Back then, people used a water wheel to create enough power to grind grain. Powerful rushing water flowed over the wheel, pushing it until it turned. This practice continued well into the nineteenth century when water wheels were used in factories to power machines for manufacturing.

Toward the end of the nineteenth century, water was being used to create electricity. The first power plant was in Niagara Falls. This famous waterfall is located on the border between New York and Canada. Scientists realized that they could use the power of the rushing water to turn a turbine. A turbine is an engine with blades that spin from water pressure. When the water passes through the turbine, it generates electricity. The more water that moves through the system, the more electricity it generates. Once the electricity is produced it can be carried long distances over electric lines to power homes and businesses. The hydropower in Niagara Falls was first used to power street lamps.

Hydropower is a cheap way to get energy. Once a hydropower plant is set up, the water to run it is free. It is also good for the environment. No chemicals are used to create the energy that comes from the water, and no toxic fumes are released into the air.

Unfortunately, building these plants in rivers and oceans can be harmful to fish. The fish often have trouble getting over the dam used to control the water. To help solve this problem, scientists are trying to come up with ways to help the fish get over or around the dams. One idea they have come up with is to build a fish ladder next to a dam.

Today, China produces more hydropower than any other country, followed by Canada, Brazil, and the United States. The biggest hydro plant in the United States is located in the state of Washington.

Use the words from the word bank to complete each sentence.

Greek	water	vapor	Niagara Falls	engine
ancient	street lamps	fish	Washington	factories

1. Hydropower comes from the force of moving _____ .

2. The word *hydro* means "water" in _____ .

3. When the sun heats water in the ocean, it turns to _____ .

4. The use of hydropower dates back to _____ times.

5. In the nineteenth century, water wheels were used in _____ to power machines.

6. The first power plant was in _____ .

7. A turbine is an _____ with blades that spin from water pressure.

8. The hydropower in Niagara Falls was first used to power _____ .

9. Building plants in rivers and oceans can be harmful to _____ .

10. The biggest hydro plant in the United States is in _____ .

The Bill of Rights

In 1787, the founding fathers of our nation gathered to write the US Constitution. In order for the Constitution to become law, the leaders of all thirteen states had to sign it. After reading it, they felt the Constitution needed to be more specific. There was nothing in it that protected the individual rights of the people. Some of these men worried that the federal government would become too powerful. It was clear that more work needed to be done. Under the leadership of James Madison, Congress prepared ten amendments to the Constitution. These ten amendments were approved in 1791 and became known as the Bill of Rights.

First: People have freedom to practice any religion they choose. It also gives them the right to free speech, freedom of the press, and the right to protest.

Second: Citizens have a right to own weapons for defense.

Third: The government cannot place soldiers in a person's home. This was a big problem during the Revolutionary War.

Fourth: The government cannot search a person's body, property, or home without a warrant. A judge must approve the warrant, and the reason for obtaining it must be good.

Fifth: A person has the right not to testify in court. It also says that once a jury decides you are innocent, you cannot be tried for the same crime again. Additionally, this amendment says that the government cannot take private property unless the government pays for it.

Sixth: People have the right to a speedy trial. The government also cannot imprison a person without a trial. The trial has to be public and the person has the right to know why he or she has been arrested. The government must provide a lawyer for the person if one is wanted.

Seventh: Citizens have the right to a jury for certain civil cases. A civil case is a disagreement between two parties.

Eighth: It is illegal to torture a person. Also, the government cannot set bail deemed excessive. Bail is the amount of money a person has to pay to get out of jail while waiting for trial.

Ninth: People have other rights besides those listed in the Constitution.

Tenth: Anything that is not covered in the Constitution should be left up to the states to decide.

Draw a line to match each description with its amendment.

1. It is illegal to torture a person.

First

2. Anything that is not covered in the
   Constitution should be left up to the states.

Second

3. Citizens have the right to a jury for civil cases.

Third

4. People have other rights besides those listed in the Constitution.

Fourth

5. Once a jury decides a person is innocent,
   that person cannot be tried for the same crime again.

Fifth

6. All people have the right to free speech.

Sixth

7. Citizens have the right to a speedy trial.

Seventh

8. People have the right to own weapons.

Eighth

9. The government cannot place soldiers in a person's home.

Ninth

10. The government cannot search a person's body,
    property, or home without a warrant.

Tenth

Let's Explore the Grand Canyon

Do you like hiking, rafting, and camping? The Grand Canyon might be just the place to visit. Located in the Arizona desert, this canyon is now considered one of the Seven Natural Wonders of the World. This is because it has so many interesting natural features. It has narrow cliffs, winding paths, and layers upon layers of red rock. It also has extreme temperatures. In the summer, the temperature can rise above 100 degrees F (38 degrees C). In the winter, the temperature can drop below 0 degrees F (-18 degrees C).

The Grand Canyon is 277 miles (446 km) long and in some places it is 18 miles (29 km) wide. From the top edge, it is 1 mile (1.6 km) straight down! The Grand Canyon is so big that you can even see it from space. So, how was this canyon created?

More than six million years ago, the Colorado River began slowly carving out the canyon. The desert is very dry, so when it rains the extra water isn't easily absorbed into the earth. This causes the river to flood, pushing mud and sand downstream. As these sediments travel through the canyon, they erode the surrounding rock. Eventually the sediments are deposited at different locations. Over time, this sediment creates new landforms in the canyon. This process still continues today, which is why the canyon is constantly widening.

The canyon is made up of many layers of rock that have been formed over time. In the winter the water seeps into the rock and freezes. The rocks expand and crack, causing further erosion. Much of this rock is Redwall limestone. This is what gives the canyon its deep red color. Granite, sandstone, and shale are some of the other types of rock found in the canyon. These can be gray, green, violet, brown, and pink.

Scientists believe that the oldest layers of rock are approximately two billion years old. If we study the rocks, we can learn a lot about what the canyon was like all those years ago. Looking closely, you might see fossils of seashells, clams, snails, and even large fish. This tells us that the canyon was once completely under water.

Today, the Grand Canyon is a national park. More than five million people visit the canyon each year to explore its natural beauty.

Answer the questions.

1. Where is the Grand Canyon located?

_____

2. How high does the temperature get in the Grand Canyon?

_____

3. How long is the Grand Canyon?

_____

4. What is the name of the river that runs through the canyon?

_____

5. What happens to the river when it rains?

_____

6. When the river floods, what does it push downstream?

_____

7. Which rock is responsible for the red color of the canyon?

_____

8. How old do scientists think the oldest layers of the rock are?

_____

9. What tells us that the Grand Canyon was once under water?

_____

10. How many people visit the Grand Canyon each year?

_____

The Ride of Paul Revere

In the spring of 1775, the British army had set up camp in Boston. They were preparing to attack the colonists. A group called the Sons of Liberty kept a close eye on the British. This was a group of patriots who believed the colonists should be free from British rule. The Sons of Liberty knew they would have to act fast to warn the colonists that the British were coming. In the middle of the night on April 18, 1775, the British began to advance. The Sons of Liberty sent out two riders on horseback: Paul Revere, a silversmith, was sent to Lexington, Massachusetts. William Dawes, a tanner, was told to go to the same place, but to take a longer route. The hope was that at least one of the men would make it there. As they rode, both Revere and Dawes told other riders what was happening. This is how they were able to spread the word and prepare for a British attack.

The men rode at night under the cover of darkness. Just to be extra safe, they also came up with another warning system. A man named Robert Newman was told to put lanterns in the tower of the Old North Church in Boston. If the British were coming by land, he would place one lantern in the window. If they were coming by sea, he would use two lanterns.

The British began to advance by sea along the Charles River. Revere made it to Lexington and warned Samuel Adams and John Hancock, two leaders of the Massachusetts Bay Colony. Dawes arrived a half an hour later. They had good luck getting to Lexington, so they decided to keep riding to warn others. In Concord, the British troops caught up with them. Revere was captured but Dawes escaped and headed back to Lexington to help the others.

Paul Revere and William Dawes helped change history. If they hadn't been brave enough to ride through the night, the colonists would not have been prepared for the British attack.

Read each question and circle the correct answer.

1. What was Paul Revere's profession?

   a) goldsmith   **b)** butcher   **c)** silversmith

2. Where did the British set up camp?

   a) Boston   **b)** New York   **c)** New Jersey

3. Who were the Sons of Liberty?

   a) militia   **b)** patriots   **c)** blacksmiths

4. What town were Paul Revere and William Dawes riding to?

   a) Lexington   **b)** Charlestown   **c)** Boston

5. What time did the men ride?

   a) in the morning   **b)** at night   **c)** at noon

6. What did Robert Newman put in the tower of the church to help warn that the British were coming?

   a) boots   **b)** lanterns   **c)** nothing

7. How did the British advance?

   a) by land   **b)** by air   **c)** by sea

8. Who were Samuel Adams and John Hancock?

   a) leaders   **b)** soldiers   **c)** farmers

9. How much longer did it take Dawes to arrive in Lexington?

   a) ten minutes   **b)** a half hour   **c)** two hours

10. Where was Revere captured?

    a) Maine   **b)** Lexington   **c)** Concord

John Smith: Brave Adventurer

Captain John Smith was an English explorer best known for founding the Jamestown Colony in Virginia. He was also a soldier, an author, and a mapmaker.

Smith was born in 1580 in Willoughby, England. He grew up on a farm and attended school until he was a teenager. When Smith was sixteen, he decided to leave home and pursue a life of adventure. He became a soldier, traveling around Europe and fighting duels. Eventually, he was promoted to captain.

In 1602, Smith's luck ran out. The Turks captured him and sold him into slavery. Smith killed his captors and escaped. He continued to travel around Europe and North Africa until 1605, when he returned to England.

Back at home, Smith became interested in helping to colonize the Americas. He joined the Virginia Company to establish the colony of Jamestown. Ready for his next adventure, Smith set out to Virginia on one of three ships. During the trip, Smith spoke against both the English government and the captain of the ship. The captain was so angry that he charged Smith with mutiny and planned to kill him. As soon as they set ashore, the captain read the orders from the Virginia Company. It said that Smith was to be one of the leaders of the colony. The captain had no choice; he had to spare Smith's life and set him free.

The first years of colonization were not easy. Many people died of starvation and disease. They also had to worry about the Powhatan Native American tribe who lived in villages nearby. In 1607, the Powhatan captured Smith and took him to their chief. The chief planned to kill Smith. Luckily, the chief's daughter, Pocahontas, pleaded for Smith's life. The chief agreed to release Smith back to the colony.

Smith was a tough leader. He demanded that everyone work and do their share. Even though many people didn't like him, they knew that if they listened to his ideas they would survive.

In 1614, Smith decided it was time to set out on yet another adventure. He led an exploration of new territory north of the colony. Once there, he mapped out the land, naming it "New England."

In 1615, Smith went home to England to write about the colonies and his adventures in the New World. He died on June 21, 1631.

Use the words from the word bank to complete each sentence.

colonize	soldier	slavery	starvation	England
tough	Pocahontas	mutiny	write	Powhatan

1. John Smith was born in _____.

2. Smith became a _____, traveling around Europe and fighting duels.

3. The Turks captured Smith and sold him into _____.

4. Smith became interested in helping to _____ the Americas.

5. The captain of the ship charged Smith with _____.

6. Many colonists died of _____ and disease.

7. In 1607, the _____ Native Americans captured Smith.

8. The chief's daughter was _____.

9. Smith was a _____ leader.

10. Smith went home to England to _____ about the colonies and his adventures.

Answer Key

Answers to some of the pages may vary.

Page 5
1. Mount Rushmore is located in the Black Hills of South Dakota.
2. It is made out of granite.
3. Gutzon Borglum was the sculptor of Mount Rushmore.
4. Chisels, picks, and air hammers were used to carve the faces in the rock.
5. The four presidents depicted are Theodore Roosevelt, Thomas Jefferson, Abraham Lincoln, and George Washington.
6. They were chosen because of the important work they did during our country's early history.
7. Each president's head is the height of a six-story building.
8. Borglum's son took over the project.
9. The project stopped because funding ran out.
10. More than three million people visit Mount Rushmore every year.

Page 7
1. rest
2. machinery
3. five
4. protects
5. strike
6. troops
7. Monday
8. fought
9. parades
10. picnic

Page 9
1. b
2. a
3. b
4. b
5. b
6. c
7. a
8. c
9. c
10. b

Page 11
9
2
1
3
8
5
7
6
10
4

Page 13
1. false
2. false
3. false
4. true
5. false
6. true
7. false
8. true
9. true
10. true

Page 15
1. Martin Luther King Jr. Day is the third Monday in January.
2. He was born on January 15, 1929.
3. He was fifteen when he entered college.
4. He joined the National Association for the Advancement of Colored People.
5. Rosa Parks refused to give up her seat on the bus.
6. He helped lead a boycott.
7. The speech is called "I Have a Dream."
8. It took place in Washington, DC.
9. He was standing on a balcony in Memphis, Tennessee.
10. He is remembered for his hard work and how he helped change our country.

Page 17
1. earth
2. Ten
3. holes
4. surface
5. cool
6. Pacific
7. west
8. greenhouses
9. renewable
10. clean

Page 19
1. kicker
2. home plate
3. field
4. pitcher
5. infielder
6. outfielder
7. defensive team
8. ball
9. first base
10. offensive team

Page 21
1. fact
2. fact
3. fact
4. inference
5. inference
6. inference
7. fact
8. fact
9. inference
10. fact

Page 23
1. He had sixteen siblings.
2. He worked for his brother.
3. His job was an apprentice.
4. He founded a volunteer fire company.
5. He invented bifocals.
6. His most famous discovery involved electricity.
7. He helped create the Declaration of Independence.
8. He felt strongly about slavery.
9. He was eighty-four when he died.
10. More than 20,000 people attended his funeral.

Page 25
1. b
2. a
3. c
4. b
5. a
6. a
7. c
8. b
9. a
10. a

Page 27
1. dairy
2. protein
3. vegetable
4. fruit
5. grain
6. dairy
7. grain
8. vegetable
9. fruit
10. protein

Page 29
1. true
2. false
3. true
4. false
5. true
6. true
7. false
8. true
9. false
10. true

Page 31
1. 1848
2. 1869
3. 1870
4. 1890
5. 1893
6. 1896
7. 1910
8. 1916
9. 1918
10. 1920

Page 33
1. travel
2. months
3. west
4. railroad
5. investors
6. California
7. Nebraska
8. hard
9. blast
10. spike

Page 35
1. false
2. true
3. true
4. false
5. false
6. true
7. false
8. true
9. false
10. true

Page 37
1. a
2. c
3. b
4. a
5. c
6. a
7. b
8. a
9. a
10. c

Page 39
1. Maya
2. Inca
3. Aztec
4. Inca
5. Inca
6. Maya
7. Aztec
8. Inca
9. Aztec
10. Maya

Page 41
Step 4
Step 2
Step 5
Step 9
Step 3
Step 6
Step 1
Step 7
Step 10
Step 8

Page 43
1. slaves
2. Emancipation Proclamation
3. free
4. Union
5. border states
6. fight
7. freedom
8. against
9. soldiers
10. ended

Page 45
1. a
2. b
3. c
4. c
5. b
6. a
7. b
8. a
9. c
10. c

Page 47
1. false
2. true
3. true
4. false
5. true
6. false
7. true
8. true
9. false
10. true

Page 49
1. stores
2. chemicals
3. problems
4. clumsy
5. immune system
6. deep
7. deepest
8. confused
9. quickly
10. ninety

Page 51
1. sacrifice
2. appreciation
3. veteran
4. patriotism
5. dedication
6. monument
7. armistice
8. ceremony
9. identify
10. armed forces

Page 53
1. bacteria
2. protozoa
3. fungi
4. virus
5. protozoa
6. virus
7. bacteria
8. virus
9. fungi
10. bacteria

Page 55
1. The United States was an agricultural society.
2. They were farmers.
3. Machines mostly ran on steam or coal.
4. People began to move to cities.
5. It was called the Industrial Revolution.
6. England was the birthplace of the Industrial Revolution.
7. It helped change the transportation industry.
8. People were investing in business.
9. The telegraph made communication easier.
10. People were forced to work in poor conditions.

Page 57
1. true
2. true
3. true
4. true
5. false
6. false
7. true
8. true
9. false
10. true

Page 59
Step 9
Step 10
Step 8
Step 3
Step 5
Step 1
Step 2
Step 6
Step 4
Step 7

Page 61
1. b
2. a
3. c
4. a
5. b
6. a
7. a
8. b
9. c
10. b

Page 63
1. Erosion
2. obstacle
3. rough
4. smooth
5. taller
6. collapse
7. subaqueous
8. erg
9. beach grass
10. sandfish

Page 65
1. Southern plantations grew cotton, sugarcane, tobacco, and rice.
2. People were protesting slavery.
3. There was less of a need for enslaved people because people lived in big cities.
4. The Abolitionist Movement was formed.
5. It means "to be set free."
6. The Underground Railroad helped to free enslaved people.
7. Frederick Douglass
8. John Brown led the raid.
9. John Brown was charged with treason.
10. The Thirteenth Amendment ended slavery.

Page 67
1. false
2. true
3. false
4. true
5. true
6. false
7. false
8. true
9. false
10. true

Page 69
1. executive
2. legislative
3. judicial
4. executive
5. legislative
6. judicial
7. legislative
8. executive
9. judicial
10. executive

Page 71
1. onion
2. outer
3. crust
4. 84 percent
5. two
6. sun
7. nickel
8. melt
9. molten lava
10. wind

Page 73
1. 1743
2. 1767
3. 1768
4. 1769
5. 1772
6. 1776
7. 1779
8. 1796
9. 1801
10. 1826

Page 75
1. b
2. a
3. b
4. b
5. c
6. a
7. a
8. c
9. a
10. b

Page 77
1. flat
2. ten
3. doormat
4. rain
5. buffalo
6. shelter
7. pioneers
8. plowed
9. cattle
10. windmills

Page 79
1. They found wheat harder to grow than corn.
2. They had to dry and store it.
3. They used a mortar and pestle.
4. You have to set the oven to 425 degrees F (218 degrees C).
5. You are supposed to use 1 ½ cups of milk.
6. You add an egg to the bowl in step 4.
7. The recipe calls for 1 tablespoon of baking powder.
8. You will need to use your measuring spoons in steps 7, 8, and 9.
9. The last step asks you to mix all the ingredients together.
10. You are supposed to bake the muffins for eighteen minutes or until they turn a golden color.

Page 81

1. true
2. false
3. true
4. true
5. false
6. true
7. true
8. true
9. false
10. false

Page 83

1. a
2. b
3. c
4. a
5. b
6. c
7. b
8. c
9. a
10. b

Page 85

1. water
2. Greek
3. vapor
4. ancient
5. factories
6. Niagara Falls
7. engine
8. street lamps
9. fish
10. Washington

Page 87

1. Eighth
2. Tenth
3. Seventh
4. Ninth
5. Fifth
6. First
7. Sixth
8. Second
9. Third
10. Fourth

Page 89

1. The Grand Canyon is located in Arizona.
2. It gets to be more than 100 degrees F (38 degrees C).
3. It is 277 miles (446 km) long.
4. The Colorado River runs through the canyon.
5. When it rains, the river floods.
6. When the river floods, sand and mud are pushed downstream.
7. Redwall limestone is responsible for the red color of the canyon.
8. Scientists think the oldest layers of rock are two billion years old.
9. The fossils tell us that the Grand Canyon was once under water.
10. More than five million people visit the Grand Canyon each year.

Page 91

1. c
2. a
3. b
4. a
5. b
6. b
7. c
8. a
9. b
10. c

Page 93

1. England
2. soldier
3. slavery
4. colonize
5. mutiny
6. starvation
7. Powhatan
8. Pocahontas
9. tough
10. write

Image Credits